Let's Learn How to Learn

Workshops for Key Stage 2

Published by Network Educational Press Ltd.
PO Box 635
Stafford
ST16 1BF

First published 2004
© UFA 2004

ISBN 1 85539 097 3

Every effort has been made to contact copyright holders of material reproduced in this book. The
publishers apologize for any omissions and will be pleased to rectify them at the earliest opportunity.
Please see page 263 for a comprehensive list of acknowledgements.

Most of the ideas and activities in this book have grown out of work the UFA have done with their
partners across the country through the UFA national programme. Ideas and activities grow and change
over time and it is not always possible to trace the 'journey of an idea' but the UFA would like to
acknowledge the valuable contribution of the UFA partnership managers and their UFA teams to this
book.

The UFA would particularly like to thank the staff and young people at the following schools and
centres who trialled these workshops and provided valuable feedback:

Moston Lane Primary School, Manchester; The Willows Primary School, Manchester; Ladybarn Primary
School, Manchester; Crab Lane Primary School, Manchester; Baguley Hall Primary School, Manchester;
St Gerards Catholic Primary School, Rotherham; Maggie Steele, The Try Line Centre, Rotherham Rugby
Football Club; Kirkheaton Primary School, Huddersfield; St John's CE J/I School, Huddersfield.

The UFA would also like to especially thank Bernie Doherty from Wharrier School Newcastle for the
songs featured in the book.

Contributors: UFA National Team (Stephen Rogers, Sarah Burgess, Manjit Shellis, Sue Barnes,
                  Lyn Reynolds, Linda Gregory, Dr Alan Jones)
Edited by: Rosalind Beckman, Lily Martin
Design by: Kim Sillitoe, Neil Hawkins
Illustrations by: Louise Gardner

Printed in Great Britain by MPG Books Ltd, Bodmin, Cornwall

Contents

Foreword   4

Introduction   5

A quick guide to the UFA   6

My amazing brain!   9
    Part 1   14
    Part 2   28
    Resource material 45

The power of positive thinking   78
    Part 1   82
    Part 2   98
    Resource material 112

Learning in different ways   130
    Part 1   134
    Part 2   144
    Resource material 155

My mega memory!   174
    Part 1   178
    Part 2   194
    Resource material 207

Mind mapping magic!   210
    Part 1   216
    Part 2   226
    Resource material 237

Super Learning Days   242
  Case studies   255

Recommended reading   261

Useful websites   262

Acknowledgements   263

Foreword

We are continually reaching out and finding out more and more about our universe. While some look out and beyond, others are driving forward the inner exploration of how and why we learn. The science of the brain has probably as many, if not more, unknowns and mysteries to uncover as the exploration of the wider universe. Who knows, the two directions may have more in common than we think.

We have to be careful in applying what we know about the science of the brain to the daily lives of our young learners. What we know about neurons at one level of complexity does not necessarily map into the curiosities and puzzles of learning and consciousness. However, it seems inconceivable that we should ignore the research altogether. We would also be foolish to ignore the wisdom accumulated by generations of teachers, parents and mentors of all kinds, who have been striving to 'make a difference'. In addition, many of our insights, whether we realize it or not, come from the works of artists, philosophers, psychologists, sociologists and those branches of human knowledge that puzzle over and attempt to illuminate one of the greatest mysteries of all: how do we learn?

There will certainly be more than one answer to this question. This publication is our contribution to the exploration and, in so doing, we are making a difference to young learners' opportunities for success in life. Brain research continues to march on apace – what we know about this amazing organ changes almost daily. Our challenge in the UFA is to use what we know now and test it out within our strong tradition of action research. Through our partnerships and the many UFA fellows who have been experimenting with these ideas and putting them into practice, we have accumulated much wisdom while recognizing how far we still have to journey.

Use this book as a voyage of discovery, safe in the knowledge that these activities, which have been practised in our schools and communities across the country, have made an impact upon the well-being of young people. The activities will not only make a difference, but they are also great fun. The UFA has learned, quite simply, that we need to get the relationships and the emotional environment right. The new science of the brain is confirming what many of you probably already know and have practised for a long time.

However you choose to use this book, feel free to adapt it to make it meaningful for yourselves – and let us know how successful you have been. Good luck!

Steve Rogers

Stephen Rogers
Director, University of the First Age

Introduction

This book has come about following the success of *Brain Friendly Revision*, which was mainly written for those working with KS3–4. Some primary colleagues have adapted the workshop activities in *Brain Friendly Revision* for use with younger children, but many have been asking for material focusing on learning to learn at KS2. So it was with this brief that we started writing *Let's Learn How to Learn*.

The workshops have been planned to model the best of what we know about learning. They have been trialled nationally across the UFA network by primary teachers in the classroom, with very positive results.

Some teachers work in mainstream schools but many work with young people in other contexts, so these materials have been designed with a range of abilities in mind. They could form the basis of learning to learn sessions during the school day, in out-of-hours clubs or Super Learning Days.

UFA Super Learning Days are one of the hallmarks of UFA partner schools and organizations. Typically, this is a day when the timetable is suspended in order to explore learning to learn strategies. The final section of this book looks at Super Learning Days in more detail, with guidance on how to set up and run a Super Learning Day and case studies showing how some of our partner schools have successfully organized them.

Using the book

There are five workshops, each split into two parts: the first part acts as a simple introduction to the topic, while the second part offers more in-depth material. Each part is comprised of several activities and will occupy about an hour to an hour and a half. The workshops can be used in any order as stand-alone units, or put together to form a Super Learning Day.

💬 Throughout the activities, a small speech bubble is used to indicate when the text should be directed at the children. You can choose whether to read the text directly to the children, or put it into your own words.

Each workshop comprises:

- an introduction
- two Family challenge sheets to encourage children to share their learning with people at home. These can also be found on the accompanying CD-ROM
- an 'at a glance' workshop plan for both Part 1 and Part 2, to give an overview of each workshop
- detailed notes for each activity, including an explanation of the overall aim, resources required and a concluding 'points to make' checklist
- photocopiable resources at the end of each workshop to support activities. These can also be found on the accompanying CD-ROM, several in colour as well as in black and white, giving you the facility to print them out to enhance the activities
- motivational posters on left-hand pages, featuring 'brain bulbs', that can be photocopied and used to enhance your learning environment or given to children to use at home. These can also be found on the accompanying CD-ROM.

We hope you enjoy exploring the learning process with the young people you work with.

A quick guide to the UFA

The UFA is a national education charity. Founded in Birmingham in 1996 by Professor Tim Brighouse, it is now working with 40 local education authorities and other partners across the UK.

> 66 *Giving young people more time to do more of the same, in the same way, with the same people is not going to raise standards of achievement dramatically upward – we need to do something radically different.* 99
>
> Professor Tim Brighouse at the launch of the UFA

The UFA has the following defining features:

- **Beyond school**
  The UFA extends the learning of young people beyond the traditional school day by offering learning opportunities before and after school, at weekends and during the holidays.

- **Networked**
  The UFA works with schools and communities to develop home, school and community linked learning programmes. Partner schools and organizations subscribe to the UFA core principles upon entering the partnership and embark on a developmental programme to enhance, extend and enrich the learning of young people.

- **Innovative**
  The UFA is committed to exploring innovative, brain-based approaches to learning to boost learner potential and raise achievement.

- **Energetic**
  The UFA is developed by energetic UFA Fellows who come from partner schools and organizations. They take part in training and work together to develop UFA activity in their own organizations and across a local area.

- **Partnership**
  The UFA works at a local level, alongside a local UFA manager, to set up partnerships with schools, community groups and other organizations in order to build the UFA network. The UFA is committed to building local capacity and uniting people, young and old, in a common endeavour to release learning potential.

U.F.A. Let's Learn How to Learn

- **Belonging**
  UFA tutors and students from UFA partner schools are brought together with other members of local UFA learning teams to build a sense of identity and a common approach to teaching and learning.

- **Transforming**
  The UFA works with schools to develop experimental, creative approaches to learning that support their commitment to transform teaching and learning for students and teachers.

66 *UFA has become a pioneer of new ways of learning – not seeking to banish or denigrate existing forms of provision, but reconfiguring resources to gain greater leverage from learning potential.* 99

Tom Bentley, DEMOS

66 *The UFA is one of the most important developments in Education at the present time.* 99

Ted Wragg, Chair of the UFA

Do you want to find out more?

Visit our website at www.ufa.org.uk to find out more about the partnership programme, the work of the UFA and how we can work with you.

email us: ufa_admin@birmingham.gov.uk

Phone us: 0121 202 2347

Fax us: 0121 202 2384

Or write to us:
    National UFA
    Millennium Point
    Curzon Street
    Birmingham
    B4 7XG

Children Learn What They Live

Dorothy Law Nolte

If children live with criticism, they learn to condemn.

If children live with hostility, they learn to fight.

If children live with fear, they learn to be apprehensive.

If children live with pity, they learn to feel sorry for themselves.

If children live with ridicule, they learn to feel shy.

If children live with jealousy, they learn to feel envy.

If children live with shame, they learn to feel guilty.

If children live with encouragement, they learn confidence.

If children live with tolerance, they learn patience.

If children live with praise, they learn appreciation.

If children live with acceptance, they learn to love.

If children live with approval, they learn to like themselves.

If children live with recognition, they learn it is good to have a goal.

If children live with sharing, they learn generosity.

If children live with honesty, they learn truthfulness.

If children live with fairness, they learn justice.

If children live with kindness and consideration, they learn respect.

If children live with security, they learn to have faith in themselves and
in those about them.

If children live with friendliness, they learn the world is a nice place in
which to live.

 Let's Learn How to Learn

My amazing brain!

"When you start to learn like this, you realize that you really *have* got a brain, and you really *can* do it. It helped my confidence."

UFA student

Introduction

Research into the brain is amassing at an incredible rate. New discoveries about the brain and the way in which it works continue to inform our knowledge, and help us to plan and facilitate more effective learning experiences for children and young people. Children will be better able to make more of their potential if they have a greater understanding of how we learn, and appreciate how several different factors affect our learning, including what we eat and drink, the amount of sleep we get, stress and the brain's response to different stimuli.

The activities in the workshops raise some of these issues, ask important questions, and reveal what some of the research is telling us about the brain and how this knowledge might help us to make our learning more effective.

There have been lots of statistics banded about regarding how much of our brain we use, for instance, the myth that we use only 10 per cent of our brain. The reality is we don't know. However, it is generally believed that we underestimate the potential we have, and sometimes we fail to inspire children with a sense of awe and wonder about their own potential. One of the main aims of this book is to do just that, to introduce children to the mind-boggling power they have inside their heads. We want children to become excited and amazed at their brain's potential, and begin to understand how to learn more effectively as a result.

Another main aim of the workshop, and one that runs throughout the book, is to help children to understand how vital their attitude and emotional state are for learning. There is so much that we don't know, and new findings continue to excite and amaze us. But some signposts from science give credence to what good teachers have always known: every child is capable of achieving success, and their emotional state is crucial to effective learning.

This workshop builds on what we currently understand about the brain and learning: the importance of colour, music and movement; the need for a positive 'I can' attitude; a greater understanding of how to think and learn. All these are important if children are going to be able to take control and direct their own learning journey.

The brain breaks on page 13 can be used at any time throughout any of the workshops, and are particularly useful when children's attention is beginning to wane. We recommend you try one out every 20 to 30 minutes to keep brains focused, so please dip back into this page whenever you feel the need.

> **!** *Don't forget to experiment with brain breaks (see page 13) – either at the start of the session or after about 20 minutes.*

Be amazed by your brain power!

Brain breaks

Brain breaks are a quick and effective way of changing or focusing the physical and mental state of learners in your group. They are a useful tool to use either at the beginning of a session or when attention starts to flag. Many schools have now integrated the use of brain breaks and other similar break-state activities into classes, and find that attention improves and children focus back on their work more readily.

In his book, *Brain-Based Learning* (1996), Eric Jensen explains that recent brain research has uncovered a strong link between movement and the brain, notably that:

- Physical stimulation boosts mental stimulation.
- Learning done with the body is generally more effective than with the mind only.
- The engagement of emotions increases the impact and recall of learning experiences.

Alistair Smith (2002) confirms this:

> *One benefit of frequent structured physical reprieve is the release of more oxygen up into the brain. Simply by standing up this process begins. Stooping and sitting are the two postures which most aggravate back pain. Stasis fatigue – stuck for too long sitting – is real. When you get children up and out of their seats you advantage their learning.*

Alistair Smith, *Move It*

The following are some examples of brain breaks from Alistair Smith's book, *Move It*. These should be interspersed throughout a session rather than done all at once, and performed in a slow, deliberate manner rather than quickly.

Super Swapper
With your right thumb and forefinger pinch your nose; with your left thumb and forefinger pinch your right ear. Now swap so that with your right thumb and forefinger you pinch your left ear, and with your left thumb and forefinger you pinch your nose.

Cross Crawler
From standing, begin to march slowly. As you raise your knees, touch them with the opposite hand.

Morecambe and Wise
With your right hand touch the heel of your left foot behind you, and then with your left hand touch the heel of your right foot. Carry on slowly. Now try to alternate Morecambe and Wise with Cross Crawler.

Double Bubble
With each hand in the air draw imaginary bubbles of different sizes as they float up. Try drawing different shapes, the letters of the alphabet, your name or words you need to remember. This can help make difficult spellings memorable. Practise with one hand to start off with and then both hands. Then, on successful completion, place the drawn image in the upper left field of vision and then try to write it with the eyes closed.

Family challenge

I know some things about my brain. Can I tell you about them?

I know how many brain cells there are in a brain. What's this number: 100,000,000,000?

I can do some exercises that will help me to concentrate and learn better – let's do them together!

Take it home – let's learn together!

Part 1: **Workshop plan**

By the end of this workshop children will:

- be excited and amazed at their brain's potential

- understand more about their brain and know how to use this understanding to help with their learning

- understand how important it is to have personal self-belief and a positive attitude in their learning

- have taken part in a number of different brain-break exercises, and understand how and when to use them.

The big idea
Your brain is awesome, amazing, powerful!

Activity 1: True/false runaround
(warm-up activity – 15 minutes)

Activity 2: Wow! What power I have!
(15 minutes)

Activity 3: Building a living brain
(20–30 minutes)

Activity 4: What have we learned?
(10 minutes)

Family challenge
Take it home – let's learn together!

Don't forget to experiment with brain breaks (see page 13) – either at the start of the session or after about 20 minutes.

Brains love colour.

Brains love pictures.

Activity 1: **True/false runaround**

Aim:	To begin to find out about our brains in an active way.
Resources:	Two labels for the walls: 'True' and 'False' (pages 45–46); plenty of space.
Time:	15 minutes.

Read out one of the statements in bold from the list below. Once the statement has been read out and the instruction 'Runaround!' has been given, the children have to run either to the 'True' wall or the 'False' wall. You can then give them the answer and explanation below each statement.

You can carry on learning throughout your life, even when you're old!
True. 'Use it or lose it' – just as you exercise to keep your body fit, you can keep learning as long as your brain is stimulated.

Bigger brains are better brains.
False. It's not the size of your brain that's important, it's how you use it that counts! Apparently, Einstein had a relatively average-sized brain, so we all have an amazing capacity to learn.

Colour and music can help your brain to learn.
True. Colour and music can help you to learn. Try using colours to colour code your work, and experiment with playing certain types of music when you are learning – it might help you to concentrate and remember.

Some people are just born 'brainier' than others.
False. Everybody is different. Everyone's brain is different. Everyone is brainy. Anyone can be brainy if they want to be! What other words mean the same as brainy? How about 'intelligent'? Although we don't fully understand yet, some scientists believe you can learn how to be more intelligent – the more you use your brain, the better it gets.

Brains are made up mostly of water.
True. To function at its best, the brain needs lots of water. Drink plenty of fresh water rather than tea, coffee or sweet, fizzy drinks, which actually dehydrate the brain. If you feel thirsty, you are already dehydrated.

Your brain likes chips, other fatty foods and sugary drinks.
False. You may like these things, but your brain will be healthier and work better on a diet of fresh fruit, vegetables and protein. Some fats are important, too. The kind of fats that are good for your brain are found in fish, nuts and grains.

Brains can be exercised.
True. Just as exercising keeps your body fit and well, your brain can be exercised too! There are exercises called brain breaks that will stimulate your brain and help it to work effectively (*see page 13*). Getting enough exercise is also important for learning.

Workshop

Brains love movement.

Brains love music.

■ Activity 1: **True/false runaround** *(continued)*

💬 **This exercise will help you to remember things about the brain.**

True. It will help you to know about your brain and how it works. It is also useful to be active when you're learning. If you get more oxygen to your brain, you are more likely to remember what you are actively involved in.

💬 **Having a positive attitude is important for learning.**

True. Your attitude is *really* important when learning. If you think you can do something, you are more likely to be able to do it. Saying 'I can do it!' to yourself really helps.

💬 **Getting enough sleep is important for learning.**

True. Recent research suggests that many children (one in eight) don't get enough sleep (the recommendation for six year olds is 11 hours). Having a TV/video in your bedroom doesn't help. You should try to go to bed at the same time every night to get your body into a regular routine.

Points to make

✓ It's great to move about when you learn – movement gets oxygen to the brain and helps you to stay alert.

✓ Would this activity have been as interesting if we had been sitting down and putting our hands up for true/false answers?

✓ Later, we'll think about how we can use what we know about the brain to help us become better learners.

Variations

If there isn't enough space for the whole group to move from one side of the room to the other, you could seat everyone in a circle. Ask them to stand up and change places if they think the statement is true.

Workshop

Did you know
you have
100,000,000,000
brain cells?

Imagine
your
potential!

Activity 2: **Wow! What power I have!**

Aim:	To raise awareness of the amazing raw capacity we all have for learning. Our huge numbers of brain cells are just waiting for us to help them to fire electric pulses and wire up together.
Resources:	Cards making up the number 100 billion. You will need one copy of card '1' (page 47) and eleven copies of card '0' (page 48).
Time:	15 minutes.

We only use a fraction of our brain's potential. Imagine what we could do if we used more! We are born with an enormous capacity to learn. At birth we have approximately 100 billion (100,000,000,000) brain cells called neurons.

100,000,000,000

Create a visual representation of this number, using volunteers. You could build it up one digit at a time, starting with the number 1.

As the children come to the front and create new numbers (1, 10, 100, and so on, building up to 100 billion), with each new number ask them, 'What is this number?' If no one knows what the final number is, set them the challenge of finding out by the end of the day.

Do we use our brain's potential?

Imagine the room is a giant brain and each child is a brain cell (neuron). Ask about a third of the children to stand up and 'connect' to each other in some way (for example, holding hands, miming sending an electronic pulse to each other, or even chatting to each other or saying the word 'connecting'). These children represent the percentage of cells that are connected to each other at birth. The rest of the children will be the part of the brain that is not yet fully wired up. Ask the children to look around the room and see how many people are standing and how many are sitting down still. Now ask the rest of the room to stand up and get everyone connected to each other – can they see the difference? If you've asked the children to talk to each other to show the connections, you'll hear the difference, too.

◼️▤ *Points to make* ▤▤▤▤▤▤▤▤▤▤▤▤▶

✓ When neurons are stimulated, they connect together. The more brain cells we can connect together, the more we are using our brain power. At birth, only a third of our cells are connected – the rest are just waiting for our brains to be stimulated by new learning.

✓ We use only a small part of our brain power, but the amount of possible connections between neurons is virtually limitless.

✓ Everyone has enormous untapped potential. By finding out about our brains, we can learn to use them better and unlock more of our potential. We can do this only if we find out more about how our brains work and what our individual ways of learning are.

Brain fact

We are all different. Our brains are as individual as our fingerprints. So, what works for one person will not necessarily work for another.

 Workshop

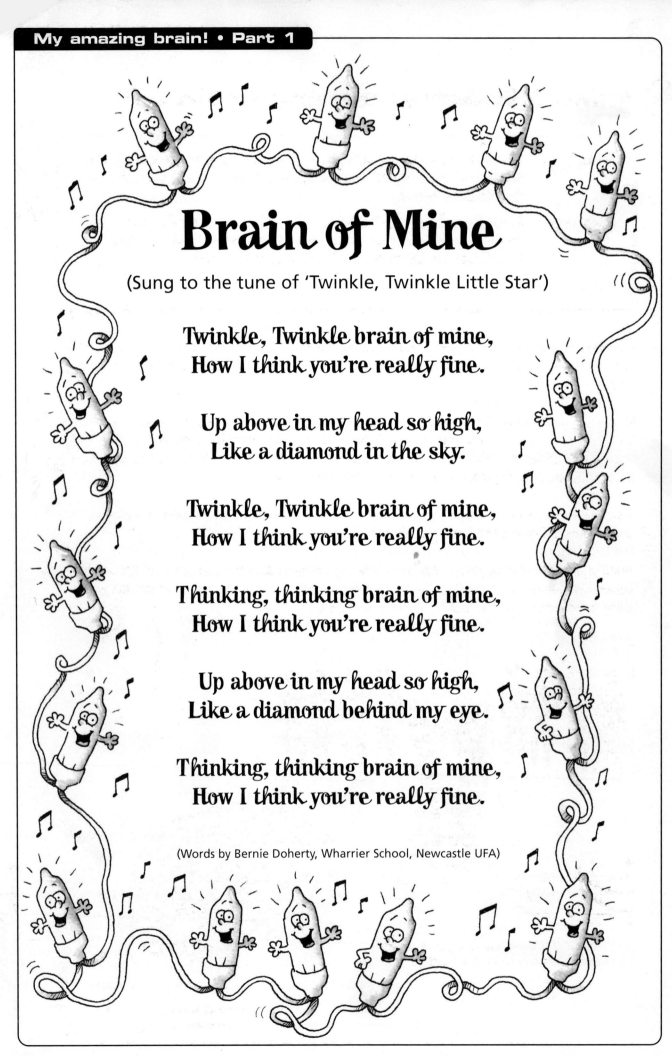

Brain of Mine

(Sung to the tune of 'Twinkle, Twinkle Little Star')

Twinkle, Twinkle brain of mine,
How I think you're really fine.

Up above in my head so high,
Like a diamond in the sky.

Twinkle, Twinkle brain of mine,
How I think you're really fine.

Thinking, thinking brain of mine,
How I think you're really fine.

Up above in my head so high,
Like a diamond behind my eye.

Thinking, thinking brain of mine,
How I think you're really fine.

(Words by Bernie Doherty, Wharrier School, Newcastle UFA)

U.F.A. Let's Learn How to Learn

Activity 3: **Building a living brain**

Aim:	A visual, kinesthetic activity to illustrate the structure of the brain and illuminate some key messages about how the brain learns effectively.
Resources:	Lots of volunteers; 'Building a living brain' script (pages 49–51); copies of the 'Building a living brain' cards to label the different parts of the brain (pages 52–63).
Time:	20–30 minutes.

This exercise will give children some basic understanding of the brain. However, it is important to note that this structure is over-simplified and research tells us that the brain is more complex than this.

It is not always possible to locate specific skills and functions in particular parts of the brain; rather they are the result of many different parts of the brain working together. Some of the best learning combines different sorts of stimuli – we remember advertising slogans and songs because the combination of language, music and rhythm is memorable.

Ask for volunteers who, through action and mime, will construct a simple model of the brain, showing its different parts and some of their functions.

Build up the model in stages, as shown in the diagram below and the chart on page 25, and then set the whole brain working together through movement or mime. You may find the 'Building a living brain' script a useful starting point for doing this.

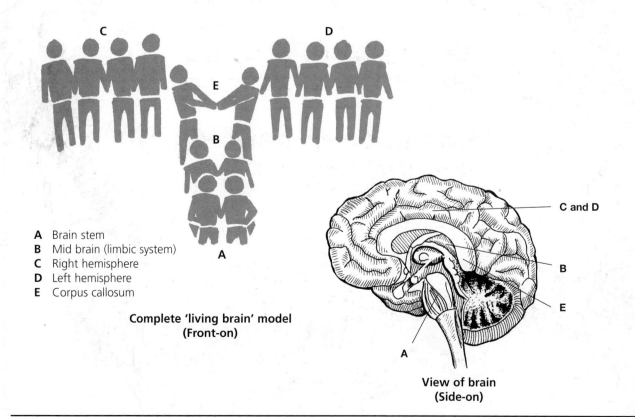

A Brain stem
B Mid brain (limbic system)
C Right hemisphere
D Left hemisphere
E Corpus callosum

**Complete 'living brain' model
(Front-on)**

**View of brain
(Side-on)**

Workshop

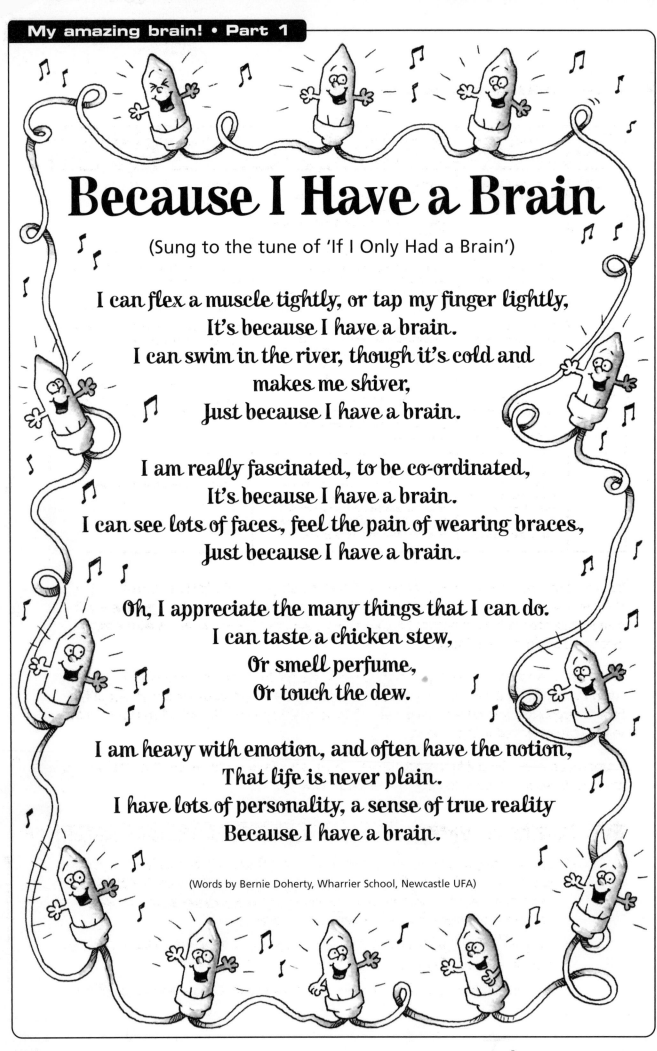

Because I Have a Brain

(Sung to the tune of 'If I Only Had a Brain')

I can flex a muscle tightly, or tap my finger lightly,
It's because I have a brain.
I can swim in the river, though it's cold and
makes me shiver,
Just because I have a brain.

I am really fascinated, to be co-ordinated,
It's because I have a brain.
I can see lots of faces, feel the pain of wearing braces,
Just because I have a brain.

Oh, I appreciate the many things that I can do.
I can taste a chicken stew,
Or smell perfume,
Or touch the dew.

I am heavy with emotion, and often have the notion,
That life is never plain.
I have lots of personality, a sense of true reality
Because I have a brain.

(Words by Bernie Doherty, Wharrier School, Newcastle UFA)

Activity 3: **Building a living brain** (continued)

No. of children	Positioning	Role and function	Mime (where appropriate)
♀ to ♀♀	Kneeling side by side, facing forwards	**A. Brain stem** Controls body functions such as breathing/heart rate and is responsible for instincts, for example fight/flight.	Mime could depict a person or animal fighting or fleeing.
♀♀	Kneeling side by side behind brain stem, facing forwards	**B. Mid brain (limbic system)** Important for long-term memory, also important for processing emotions	One child to mime emotion, the other to mime memory.
♀♀♀ to ♀♀♀♀	Standing and facing forwards on right side (left as you're looking at it!)	**C. Right hemisphere** Responsible for: music, creativity, visual/spatial skills. Looks at the Big Picture.	Ask each volunteer to think of a mime for each of these functions.
♀♀♀ to ♀♀♀♀	Standing and facing forwards on left side (right as you're looking at it!)	**D. Left hemisphere** Responsible for: language, logic, analysis and detail. Takes activities step by step.	Ask each volunteer to think of a mime for each of these functions.
♀♀	Standing in between left and right hemispheres, facing each other and linking arms across top of mid-brain (B)	**E. Corpus callosum** Bundle of fibres connecting left and right hemispheres – they send electrical signals back and forth so that the left and right sides can 'talk to each other' and work as one.	Sway back and forth to show communication between left and right.

You could use the resource sheets (pages 52–63) at this stage to make 'picture medals' for the children to wear, by simply punching holes in the sheets and passing string through. These will help to illustrate the brain functions for children who are more visually aware, as each sheet belongs to a part of the living brain.

Finally, you can ask the remaining children to join in the fun by getting them to swap with children currently making up the living brain. They can take a moment to rehearse what that part of the brain is responsible for and what that means for the way they learn. This will allow more children to be actively involved in the process.

If space is an issue, the children could make the brain parts from plasticine, but this activity is most effective done as a group with lots of whole-body movement.

Points to make

✓ Stress stops you from learning effectively – it is difficult to think clearly when you are upset or stressed. Show this by asking everyone in the model, except the brain stem, to sit down again. The brain stem continues to make sure we survive difficult and dangerous situations, even if we can't think straight.

✓ Learning can be fun. When positive emotions are associated with learning, you will be more likely to remember it.

✓ Brain exercises/movements strengthen connective impulses across the corpus callosum.

Workshop

Make learning easier – feed your brain what it needs!

YUM!

I love fresh fruit, vegetables and fish.

I need to drink lots of water throughout the day because

it helps me to concentrate on what I'm learning.

I only have fizzy drinks and fatty foods occasionally.

U.F.A. Let's Learn How to Learn

Activity 4: **What have we learned?**

Aim:	To help the children think back over the session to what they have learned.
Resources:	None.
Time:	10 minutes.

This can be done as a pair-and-share activity, or by leading the group through a guided reflection of the session.

Ask the children to think back over the workshop. They can try to visualize scenes in their mind's eye, focus on how they have been feeling at different points, or even recall particular things that have been said.

Think about the different activities we've been doing:

- What things have we learned about our brains?

- How do you feel about what you've learned?

- What will you remember about today?

Now ask everyone to think of one word that sums up the workshop for them – it might be to do with the content of the workshop, or how they are feeling about what they have learned about their brains. Go round the group and ask each person to say their word out loud in quick succession, in a kind of domino effect. (If words are repeated, that's fine!)

Workshop

Family challenge

I know some more facts about my brain. Can I tell you about them?

Can I show you how to do some more brain breaks? They help me to concentrate.

Let me show you my speech bubble and what I felt about today.

Take it home – let's learn together!

U.F.A. Let's Learn How to Learn

Part 2: **Workshop plan**

By the end of this workshop children will have:

- further explored their amazing brains
- consolidated their knowledge about the brain
- thought about who else needs to know and why.

 The big idea
You can help your brain to work well!

Activity 5: **The learning rucksack**
(10–15 minutes)

Activity 6: **So what do I know?**
(15 minutes)

Activity 7: **So who shall I tell?**
(30-plus minutes)

Activity 8: **What I want to say**
(review activity – 10 minutes)

 Family challenge
Take it home – let's learn together!

! *Don't forget to experiment with brain breaks (see page 13) – either at the start of the session or after about 20 minutes.*

'I learned a lot today.'

UFA student

U.F.A. Let's Learn How to Learn

Activity 5: **The learning rucksack**

> **Aim:** To recap knowledge learned so far.
> **Resources:** Rucksack with a range of objects in it (see below).
> **Time:** 10–15 minutes.

This is a useful introductory activity, but works just as well as a review activity – it's also great to do in assembly. The activity will help children to develop their own 'tool kit for learning'. In the rucksack are some of the things that are important for learning, to prepare them for their 'learning journey'. What can they remember about what they have learned about their brain?

Children like the element of surprise in this activity. Invite them to come up, feel inside the rucksack and take something out. The children can stay at the front of the group holding the item they have taken out, or display it where everyone can see it. Limit the number of items to no more than ten. The sort of things you need in the rucksack are:

● **Bananas**

These are especially good brain food.

● **Bottle of water**

Hydrating the brain is essential for smart learning.

● **CD**

Music can help us to learn. Some music (especially slow Baroque music) encourages certain brain waves (alpha waves) that help the brain to learn. This is especially good for memorization.

● **Colour chart/pack of felt-tip pens**

The brain loves colour. When we need to remember something, using colour to underline and emphasize it will help.

● **Map**

We need to know where we are going; we need to set goals. The brain likes to be given the Big Picture of what we are learning and why we are learning it. (This also connects to mind mapping, an excellent tool for learning, see 'Mind mapping magic!' workshop.)

● **Length of rope**

Our brain is a social brain and needs to communicate with and talk to other brains. Use two volunteers here to hold on to either end of the rope.

● **Large cut-out smile or poster of a positive statement**

This signifies a positive outlook and attitude. If you tell your brain it can do something it is more likely to be able to do it than if it thinks it can't. Having a positive 'I can' attitude is important for learning.

Workshop

'I didn't know I was brainy.'

UFA student

U.F.A. Let's Learn How to Learn

Activity 5: **The learning rucksack** *(continued)*

● **Pillow**

Sleep is important for learning.

● **Camera**

Your brain loves pictures and can recognize up to 35,000 images per hour.

● **Trainer**

Movement is good for learning – your brain needs lots of oxygen and moving around will help. It is also important to take regular exercise.

Ask the children:

💬 How many of these things can you remember?

💬 How many of these things will you remember next week?

💬 What else would you like in your own personal learning rucksack?

Points to make

✓ We can remember visual things easily.

✓ Those who actually took something out of the rucksack are more likely to remember it for longer because they were actually involved.

Workshop

Make friends with your brain.

Find out as much as you can!

Activity 6: **So what do I know?**

Aims:
- To give children an opportunity to engage with the many brain facts they have been presented with in Part 1 of this workshop, and to demonstrate their knowledge.
- To provide an opportunity for discussion in order to make personal meaning from the learning.
- To stimulate discussion about the difference between 'needing' and 'liking'.

Resources: Envelopes containing sentence stems, words, phrases and pictures (pages 64–71). Prepare one envelope for each group of three children in advance.

Time: 15 minutes.

Brain fact

We can forget things quite quickly unless we go over our learning. This activity will help us to review what we have learned.

Give each group of three children an envelope containing the beginning of three sentences:

- Our brains like …

- Our brains dislike …

- Our brains need …

Also in the envelope are words, phrases and pictures which the children must match to the sentence beginnings to make full sentences. For those children whose reading skills are still emergent, matching the pictures to the sentence stems can be the starting point. The children can draw additional pictures to match the sentences. During this process, it is useful to encourage the children to discuss their thoughts.

After 5–10 minutes, or once most groups have done much of the matching, ask each one to join with another group to compare their answers and to discuss any differences.

Once the children have finished their sentences they may have found a similar grouping to the columns on page 37.

Workshop

Your brain needs plenty of sleep to work properly.

How much sleep do you get?

U.F.A. Let's Learn How to Learn

■ Activity 6: **So what do I know?** *(continued)*

Sentence stems:	Our brains like ...	Our brains dislike ...	Our brains need ...
Words and phrases:	colour	fizzy drinks	fresh air/oxygen
	to be relaxed	sugary and fatty foods	fresh water
	music	making mistakes	healthy food
	brain exercises		movement
	funny things/humour		enough sleep
	me smiling		breakfast
	positive thinking		time to think about our learning
	a challenge		
	sharing ideas with other people		
	happy thoughts		
	feeling successful		
	doing well		
	getting praise		
	to feel safe		
	pictures		

The categorizations above are simply guideline suggestions; many of the words and phrases can, in fact, be matched with other sentence stems, as the children may discover. At this stage, you may wish to discuss the difference between 'need' and 'like', if the group have not already raised the question.

Activity 7, 'So who shall I tell?' takes this activity a stage further.

Points to make

✓ There are many things our brain *needs* in order to be ready for effective learning, such as good nutrition and sleep.

✓ There are some things that our brains *like*, which help them to work more efficiently, such as colour and pictures.

✓ Talking about your learning, and reviewing the learning by going over it, helps to reinforce it and make it more memorable.

Variations

● Separate the lists of words into two piles – my brain's likes and dislikes.

● Put the sentence stems on to different walls. When you read out the words, the children run to the appropriate wall.

Workshop

Every brain is unique!

U.F.A. Let's Learn How to Learn

Activity 7: **So who shall I tell?**

Aims:
- To give children time to engage with what we know about the brain and consider the implications for a range of different people.
- To give them an opportunity to demonstrate their knowledge.

Resources: Three large sheets of plain paper and coloured pens for each group; instruction sheet 'Showing what I know!' (page 72); a topic sheet for each group (pages 73–76).

Time: 30-plus minutes.

The children work in small groups on one of the following topics:

- Using my body
- My feelings
- Music, colour and pictures
- Eating, drinking and sleeping

Their challenge is to think about that topic and then decide on the advice or top tips for the following groups of people:

- other children and classes
- parents, family members and carers
- teachers.

You may want to give groups a choice of topic on which to work, or you may decide to give groups particular topics.

The children can present the advice in the form of a reminder sheet, poster or advice sheet. Use the 'Showing what I know!' sheet to go through the specific requirements from each group. The challenge is to complete the group task in the time given (decide how long this is to be).

'So what do I know?' (Activity 6, page 35) is a useful introduction to this activity as it provides some pointers for those children who may need extra support to get started. Younger children may like to draw their own pictures or can be provided with pictures and words to montage together to produce a poster. The words and pictures from 'So what do I know?' can be used to build up information for the poster.

◼◼ *Points to make* ▬▬▬▬▬▶

✓ An important part of the learning process is giving your brain the chance to apply information to different contexts. You need to give your brain the chance to think about new learning and consider how that information can be used. This will help you to remember it for much longer.

✓ What we've learned about our brains will be useful for lots of different people, and we need to share it.

Workshop

U.FA. Let's Learn How to Learn

The Dendrite Song

(Sung to the tune of 'Clementine')

Use your dendrites, use your dendrites,
To connect throughout your brain.
Take in info, analyse it,
Grow some new ones unrestrained.

Axons send out neurotransmitters,
To the dendrites all around.
Across the synapse, jumps the impulse,
New ideas can now abound.

Stimulation is what the brain needs,
To make dendrites stretch and grow.
New connections make us smarter,
In what we think and what we know.

Use your dendrites, use your dendrites,
To connect throughout your brain.
Take in info, analyse it,
Grow some new ones unrestrained.

(Words by Bernie Doherty, Wharrier School, Newcastle UFA)

Activity 7: **So who shall I tell?** *(continued)*

Variations

● Feedback can be presented in a variety of ways, depending on the time you have to devote to this activity. The 'Showing what I know!' sheet can be adapted to reflect the product outcome you want.

● The three pieces of advice could be fed back as a group presentation.

● The poster or advice sheet could be replaced with a group rhyme or short poem.

● This work could form the basis of a 'class charter' for learning.

● The activity could be the start of a larger project where the group advises another class or parents, or runs an assembly for the rest of the school, using their posters for a real audience.

Workshop

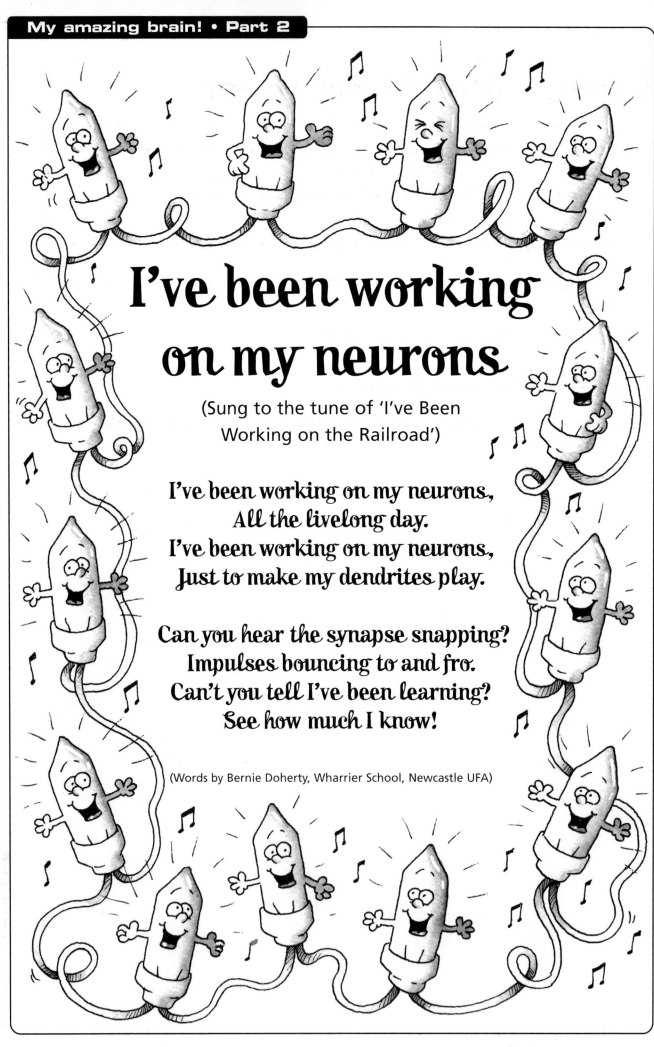

I've been working on my neurons

(Sung to the tune of 'I've Been Working on the Railroad')

I've been working on my neurons,
All the livelong day.
I've been working on my neurons,
Just to make my dendrites play.

Can you hear the synapse snapping?
Impulses bouncing to and fro.
Can't you tell I've been learning?
See how much I know!

(Words by Bernie Doherty, Wharrier School, Newcastle UFA)

Activity 8: **What I want to say**

Aim:	To reflect on the workshop and for children to think about what they have learned.
Resources:	Blank speech bubble for every child (page 77).
Time:	10 minutes.

Give each child a speech bubble and ask them to think back over the workshop, to everything they have learned about their brains.

💬 How do you feel about what you've learned?

Now ask them to talk it through with someone else.

They decide what words they would like to write in their speech bubbles to help to explain what they think.

Workshop

Don't forget...

Help your brain remember.

Go over your learning again ...

and **again**...

and **again!**

You must review your learning regularly.

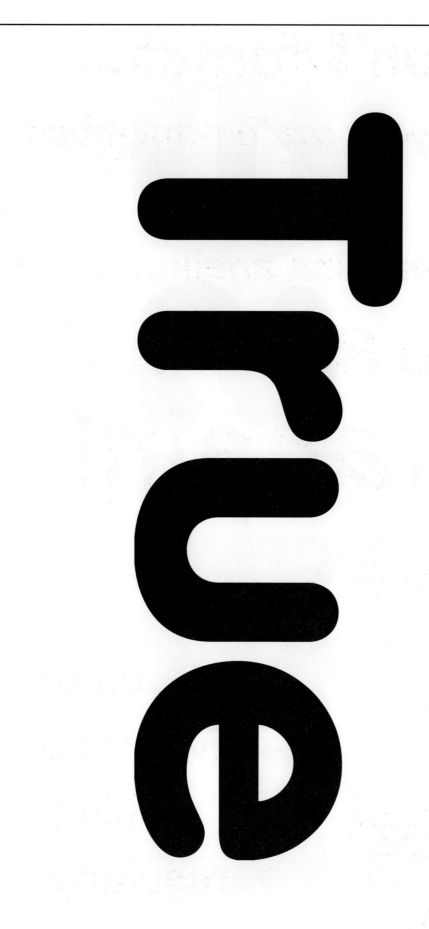

Activity 1

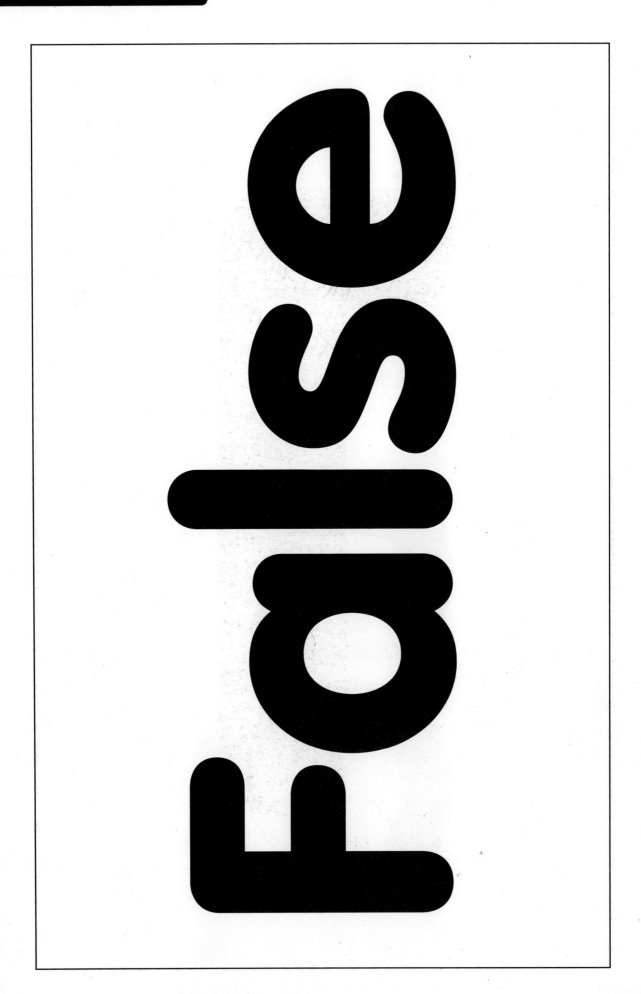

Activity 1

Activity 2

Activity 2

U.F.A. Let's Learn How to Learn

'Building a living brain' script

We're now going to make a living brain here in this room, so we'll need lots of you to volunteer to help us do this.

First of all, I'd like one or two people please to kneel down. You are the **brain stem**. You are the part of the brain that develops first — the oldest part of the brain. Your job is to keep the body alive, by regulating many life support systems such as blood pressure, digestion and breathing, and maintaining our 'fight or flight' response. Most animals have a part of their brain that does this.

Now could you please mime something that gives us an idea why this part of the brain is important. Perhaps you could mime something that shows how this part of the brain keeps the body alive, tells us when we are hungry, thirsty or tired, and makes sure we are breathing. This part of the brain is very important and we need to keep it happy — if we are hungry or thirsty, tired or worried, we will find it much harder to learn.

OK. Now we need two more people to kneel down behind the brain stem. You are the **middle part of the brain**, known as the **limbic system**. This part of the brain looks after our emotions and feelings such as sadness, happiness, boredom and fear. Could you both mime an emotion please? It's good to try and link our learning to positive emotions, as this will help us to remember.

Activity 3

Resource material

This part of the brain is important because emotions are linked to everything we do and influence our learning. We often remember things that we have found silly or funny, or lessons where the teacher has linked a joke to the learning. This part of our brain is also really important for creating and retrieving memories. Could you mime remembering things?

Now we need four people to be the **right** and four to be the **left** sides of the brain. Did you know that your brain has two halves? Each half is responsible for helping you learn in different ways. And although there are two halves, they work very closely together. Let's look at the right and the left side of the brain.

OK. First let's make the **right side of the brain**. Can you each do a mime to show some of the things this part of our brain is good at? Let's see:

- the Big Picture — seeing the whole thing
- music — playing and listening to music
- imagination — thinking creatively
- visualization — seeing.

OK. Now we need to build the **left side of the brain** and to mime:

- learning step by step — a bit at a time
- analysis — looking at things in detail
- language — words we speak, read and write
- logic — doing things in an ordered way.

Now we need to build the **corpus callosum**. This is a huge bundle of fibres that acts like a bridge connecting the left and right sides of the brain. When we do brain exercises, it is this part of the brain that we are using and strengthening, getting the left and right sides of the brain to act as one. We need two people to be the corpus callosum. Can you two turn to face each other, link hands and move backwards and forwards?

OK. Now let's see the whole brain come alive! The best sort of learning is when our brain stem is keeping us going and we are feeling good and thinking positive, `I can' thoughts. We constantly use lots of different ways of learning – for example, putting together words with pictures and music; using many parts of the brain at once.

Now I would like everyone, apart from the brain stem and middle part of the brain (the limbic system), to sit down. This is what can happen when your emotions or your need to survive a particular situation take over – the other parts of the brain are cut off. This could be because you are hungry or thirsty, when you are tired or tell yourself you can't do something, or you are angry, worried or afraid. The part of the brain that is working the hardest is the bit we cannot control – the brain stem. This makes us act according to instinct rather than reason, in ways that might not help our learning. If we learn different ways of relaxing and avoiding stress, we can stop this happening too often, and can learn better.

Thank you to our living brain for showing us how you work!

Now, can members of our audience get up and find someone to swop with? It's your turn to make a living brain!

Activity 3

Survival

Brain stem

Memory

Mid brain (limbic system)

Feelings

Mid brain (limbic system)

U.F.A. Let's Learn How to Learn

Words

Left side

Logic

Left side

Analysis

Left side

Activity 3

Left side

Step by step

Music

Right side

Activity 3

Pictures

Right side

Imagination

Right side

Activity 3

The whole picture

Right side

Activity 3

_U.F.A._ Let's Learn How to Learn

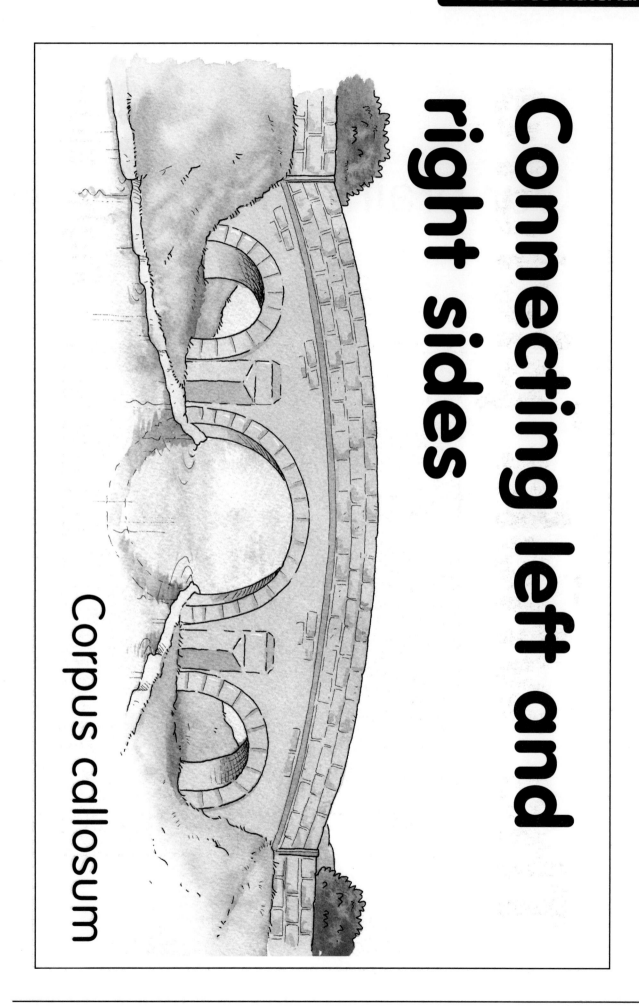

Connecting left and right sides

Corpus callosum

Our brains like ...

Our brains dislike ...

Our brains need ...

fresh air/oxygen

music

fresh water

colour

healthy food

movement

to be relaxed

a challenge

brain exercises

pictures

enough sleep

doing well

funny things/humour

fizzy drinks

getting praise

sugary and fatty foods

making mistakes

breakfast

me smiling

happy thoughts

feeling successful

time to think about our learning

sharing ideas with other people

positive thinking

to feel safe

Activity 6

Activity 6

Showing what I know!

On your desk is a sheet telling you the topic your group is going to concentrate on, as well as three large sheets of plain paper and some colouring pens.

Using the topic sheet your group has been given, design three different reminder sheets, advice sheets or posters which will explore the possible answers to the questions on the sheet.

Your group must produce one for each of the following three groups of people:

- other children/classes
- parents/family
- teachers.

Each reminder sheet, advice sheet or poster must include:

- a title or slogan
- at least three pieces of advice
- pictures and words
- at least three colours.

Within your group, you can work individually or in pairs, as long as the group as a whole produces at least three different items (you can produce more than three if you like).

Here's the challenge. You have to complete your task in the time given, which means that you have to use every minute – and everybody has to do their bit!

Good Luck!

Activity 7

Using my body

What do we know?

What can we do in school?

What can we do at home?

My feelings

What do we know?

What can we do in school?

What can we do at home?

Music, colour and pictures

What do we know?

What can we do in school?

What can we do at home?

Activity 7

Eating, drinking and sleeping

What do we know?

What can we do in school?

What can we do at home?

U.F.A. Let's Learn How to Learn

Resource material

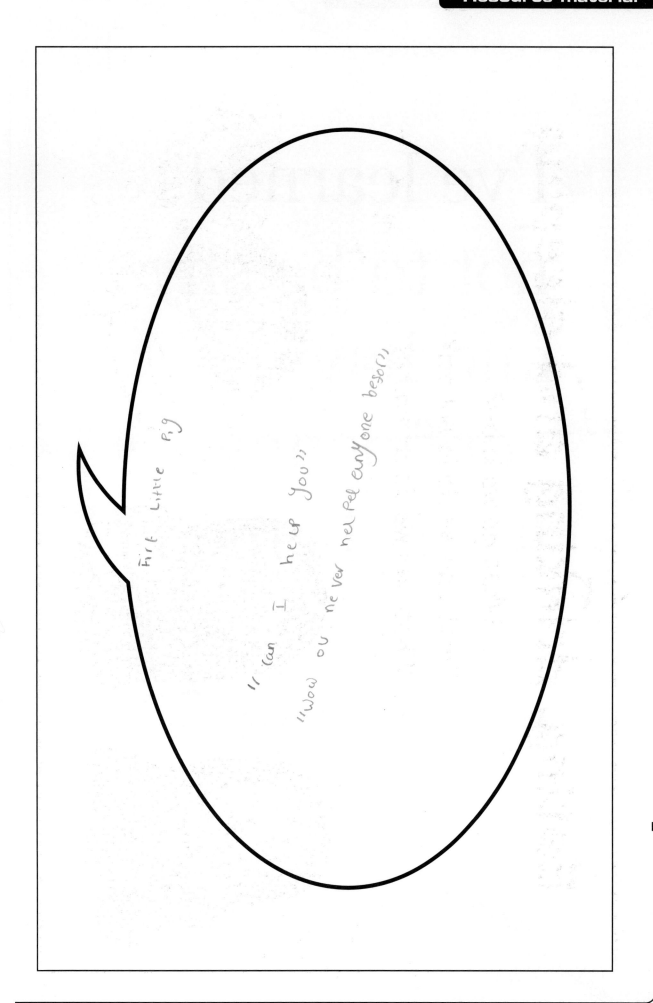

Activity 8

‘I've learned not to be shy and have confidence. It has helped me work well in a group.’

UFA student

U.F.A. Let's Learn How to Learn

The power of positive thinking

'Now I know I can do it!'

UFA student

U.F.A. Let's Learn How to Learn

Introduction

The first part of this workshop emphasizes the importance of a positive attitude for learning. The second part aims to build on this and explores how to develop a positive mental attitude. Looking at examples of human success, this part moves forward by attempting to challenge limiting self-beliefs.

This will help you and the children to think about the importance of self-talk. Our own self-talk is amazingly powerful – but that includes negative self-talk, which can quickly undermine the positive self-talk that you are trying to encourage your children to use. This is a long journey and these workshops are only the first steps: all of the activities here need reinforcement at every opportunity.

There are many ways of extending this work. You could adopt some of the quotes and posters as a group or class, so that their messages can be reinforced daily. But the most powerful way of ensuring that children adopt a positive mental attitude is to model it yourself, in the way you approach things, the way you work with others and, most importantly, the language you use.

Family challenge

Take it home – let's learn together.

Part 1: Workshop plan

By the end of this workshop children will have:

- taken part in activities promoting an 'I can' attitude
- some understanding that attitude impacts on learning.

The big idea

- 'Whether you think you can or you think you can't – you're right.'

  Henry Ford

- Me and the way I think and feel about myself affects my learning.

Activity 1: **Move and talk**
(5–10 minutes)

Activity 2: **Smiling**
(5 minutes)

Activity 3: **The power of positive thinking**
(15–20 minutes)

Activity 4: **'I can!' runaround**
(10 minutes)

Activity 5: **Positive adjectives**
(15 minutes)

Family challenge

Take it home – let's learn together!

! *Don't forget to experiment with brain breaks (see page 13) – either at the start of the session or after about 20 minutes.*

'Whether you think you can or you think you can't – you're right.'

Henry Ford

U.F.A. Let's Learn How to Learn

Activity 1: **Move and talk**

Aim:	To make children alert and focused and start them thinking and talking in a positive way.
Resources:	Circle of chairs.
Time:	5-10 minutes.

This warm-up activity is similar to Activity 6, 'Stand and change' (page 101), but everyone has to move.

First, set up a circle of chairs where the children can sit. Make sure they don't get too comfortable though, because now you're going to ask everyone to stand up, walk across the circle and sit next to someone they don't usually work with.

💬 Say 'hello' to your new neighbour, tell them something you like and explain why.

After a few minutes, it's time for the children to change places again, and sit down next to someone different.

💬 Tell your new partner about your favourite place.

After a short while, they move a third time.

💬 This time, talk about something you're good at.

You can extend this activity as much as you like, or ask the children to talk about different topics.

Workshop

Go on – smile!

U.F.A. Let's Learn How to Learn

Activity 2: **Smiling**

Aim:	For the children to experience how body position and demeanour can affect how they feel.
Resources:	None.
Time:	5 minutes.

This is a tutor-led activity that helps children understand how powerful their posture and facial expressions are as a tool for positive thinking.

Ask the children to find a space where they can sit or stand. Explain how our body posture and facial expressions can be key to whether we are thinking positively or not. Ask the children to follow your instructions (see below) as you take them through different postures and expressions, and ask them to be aware of how each one makes them feel.

> Look down, lower your chin, cast your eyes downwards, hunch your shoulders over. Now add a glum expression to this posture and frown.
>
> How do you feel?

At this point you can either ask the children to share how they are feeling or just ask them to think in their head.

> Now look up, tilt your head back as if you're looking at the sky, straighten your back so your shoulders are no longer hunched. Add a big smile, feel it relaxing your face, raise your eyebrows and get rid of that frown! Slowly take a big deep breath in, and then even more slowly let it out.
>
> How do you feel?

Smiling and laughing actually has an immediate impact on our brains. Even if we don't feel like smiling, going through this routine will help to put us in a more positive frame of mind.

This activity links straight into the next one – another visualization activity.

Workshop

No one can do everything, but everyone can do something.

Activity 3: **The power of positive thinking**

Aim:	For the children to experience a positive visualization and see how that makes a difference to the way we think and feel.
Resources:	None.
Time:	15–20 minutes.

Introduce the Henry Ford quote (page 84): 'Whether you think you can or you think you can't – you're right.' Simply put, if you believe you can do something, you are much more likely to achieve it than if you don't believe you can.

Our beliefs about what we can and can't do are complicated, built up by our experience and by what other people tell us. But the way we talk to ourselves is probably the most important thing of all. We all talk to ourselves, not out loud, but we have silent conversations with ourselves inside our heads. The way we talk to ourselves has a really big impact on what we achieve.

How well you do at something depends on:

● how you think *and*

● what you believe.

Both of these factors influence how you talk to yourself.

💬 Let's do a quick experiment. Think about a dog – a black dog – and picture it clearly. Describe it to yourself. What does it look like? What is it doing? How is it behaving?

Some of you may have had nice experiences with dogs and will, as you describe it, think nice things. If any of you has had a bad experience with a dog, you might not have such nice thoughts. If you have had a really bad experience and have been bitten by a dog, you might have had some of those uncomfortable feelings brought back to mind.

So our past experience, what we believe and how we think about different things will affect how we think and how we talk to ourselves about them.

Now we're going to try another experiment, a bit like the last one. You need to be sitting down and relaxed.

Think about a time when you felt very tired, weak and run-down. Remember that time now. Think back to what was happening to you. What were you feeling? What was going on at that time? Perhaps you felt a bit down, maybe sad, fed up or tired. Hold that memory in as much detail as you can for about 30 seconds.

Workshop

'Attitudes are contagious. Are yours worth catching?'

Anon

U.F.A. Let's Learn How to Learn

■ Activity 3: **The power of positive thinking** *(continued)*

🗩 Now try to stand up.

- How do you feel?
- What's your mood like?

OK. Now sit down again and relax.

Now think about a time when you felt really good, very happy and relaxed, perhaps full of energy, lively, bouncy and really positive. Hold that memory now and think about it. Where were you? Who were you with? What was happening? How were you feeling? Hold that memory in as much detail as you can for about 30 seconds.

Now try to stand up.

- How do you feel?
- What's your mood like?

The things you think about influence your mood, and these things influence not only the way you feel, but also how your body performs. You may have felt weaker when you remembered a time when you were unhappy, and stronger when you remembered a time when you were happy.

Performance is influenced by the way you think – your mind and body are linked!

You may want to talk this exercise through further with the group as it may have evoked very powerful memories that the children want to talk about.

🗩 One of the ways we can use this technique is to have a really positive memory to call on when we need to cheer ourselves up, feel more positive about something or even to help us go to sleep at night.

We're going to take this a step further now. Can you sit back down, close your eyes and try to think of a time when you learned to do something? It may be something you found hard at first, something you struggled with, but then managed to achieve. It can be something to do with school, but it doesn't have to be, so you might remember learning how to ride a bike, or learning to swim. I'm going to ask you some questions about your memories that I'd like you to think about:

- Where are you?
- What are you doing?
- How does it feel?
- What are you thinking and saying to yourself as you're doing it?
- Is anyone else around?
- What are they saying?

Workshop

Dream it.
Believe it.
Do it!

U.F.A. Let's Learn How to Learn

Activity 3: **The power of positive thinking** (continued)

💬 Now open your eyes. We can all achieve things and do what we want to do if we think positively. This memory might help you when you feel stuck. Remember how you felt, how we managed to do it.

'Just do it' was the slogan of a well-known sportswear company. Wouldn't it be great if achieving what we want in life was that easy? What holds us back? All of our feelings, all of the things we believe to be true are based on our internal thoughts, our self-talk. By changing our self-talk, we can change the way we see ourselves and what we believe to be possible.

One of the things we can do is change some of the language we use when we talk to ourselves. Instead of saying 'I can't', why not try saying 'I can't *yet*'. That little word is important. It means we believe that it will happen in the future. Try to make your self-talk more positive.

Workshop

I can do it!

Activity 4: 'I can!' runaround

Aim:	To consolidate the work on self-talk, and emphasize a positive way of looking at things.
Resources:	Posters for three corners of the room (pages 112–114); plenty of space.
Time:	10 minutes.

This is a fun, physical activity that will really get the positive thinking moving. Explain that the idea behind this game is to think about the things the children *can* do, and think more positively about things they can't do – *yet*.

Use a large space and put up a poster in three corners of the room:

- 'I can' (something you can already do).

- 'Not yet, but I will' (something you will be able to achieve on your own).

- 'With help I'll be able to' (something you need help with to achieve).

Ask the children to move into the middle of the room and then ask them to run to one of the three posters, depending on what you read out, for example, swimming a width of the swimming pool. Once everyone has run to the appropriate poster for their response, ask them to chat to someone near them. If they are in the 'I can' group, they might talk about how, when or where they did it. If they are in the 'Not yet, but I will' group, they might talk about how they are going to do it, how they will be more determined, and so on. If they are in the 'With help I'll be able to' group, they might talk about who they will ask to help them and, perhaps, when they are going to try again.

Other examples are below (you may need to modify these, depending on the age of the group).

Can you:

- Ride a bike without stabilizers?

- Play a musical instrument?

- Write a story?

- Recite the seven-times table?

- Bounce back when something goes wrong?

- Work as part of a team?

You could also include topical examples or things you've been working on recently.

Ask whether there were any statements that didn't apply to them? For example, perhaps they don't have any intention of learning to ride a bike. That's another example of self-talk. If you don't believe something is important, you are much less likely to get round to doing it.

Workshop

Be positive!

U.F.A. Let's Learn How to Learn

Activity 5: **Positive adjectives**

> **Aim:** To explore positive language a bit further by complimenting each other and oneself.
>
> **Resources:** Positive adjective pack, including blank cards for each pair of children (pages 115–117); a 'This is me' sheet for every child (page 118).
>
> **Time:** 15 minutes.

This isn't so much a review as an ending activity, so you may want to include a review after it to talk over all of the things you have covered in the workshop, perhaps while the children are colouring in their sheets at the end.

Working in twos, give each pair a positive adjective pack and ask them to have a look and read through it just to make sure they know what the words mean – are there any they are unsure of?

● Pair up and think about your partner. Which three words would you use to describe them? They don't have to be like the description all the time, but you may have noticed, for example, a time when they were polite. If you would like to write your own word down because it isn't on the list, then use one of the blanks. When you have made your decision, give your partner the three words you picked and say why you chose them. Now swap round and let your partner choose three words to describe you.

On the 'This is me' sheet, draw a picture of yourself or write your name in the large box. Now write the words your partner has given you in the boxes below.

Now think of three positive adjectives that you would use to describe yourself – try to think of three different ones. Remember, it doesn't have to be a description that always applies to you, and you can use the blanks to write down words that aren't in the pack. Once you have done this, add your own three words to the sheet.

Now you can spend your time colouring and decorating your sheet. As you do so, think about the things that stand out from what we've done today. Have a chat with your partner while you're colouring.

Family challenge

I've been thinking about the things I can do. Can I tell you?

I've found out about some amazing things that people have done. Can I tell you about Cliff Young?

Let me tell you about the promise I've made to myself.

Take it home – let's learn together!

U.F.A. Let's Learn How to Learn

Part 2: **Workshop plan**

By the end of this workshop children will have:

- found out about some amazing success stories
- tested their attitude towards learning
- explored how to change limiting self-talk.

The big idea

'It has been said that bumble bees aren't designed to fly … Seems like no one told them!'

Dr Alan Jones, UFA Fellow

We hold limiting self-beliefs about what we can and can't do. When these are challenged, the world opens up.

Activity 6: **Stand and change**
(10 minutes)

Activity 7: **What's your inner voice saying?**
(tutor-led role play – 10 minutes)

Activity 8: **Cliff Young's story**
(10 minutes)

Activity 9: **Agree or disagree?**
(10 minutes)

Activity 10: **Challenging my thoughts**
(20 minutes)

Family challenge
Take it home – let's learn together!

Don't forget to experiment with brain breaks (see page 13) – either at the start of the session or after about 20 minutes.

'It has been said that bumble bees aren't designed to fly ... Seems like no one told them!'

Dr Alan Jones, UFA Fellow

U.F.A. Let's Learn How to Learn

Activity 6: **Stand and change**

Aim:	To encourage the children to begin questioning the beliefs we hold about human abilities – and perhaps our own potential?
Resources:	Circle of chairs.
Time:	10 minutes (but can be shorter or longer depending on discussion).

This starter activity could be done as a paper exercise, but is much more fun, memorable and stimulating if done as a group.

The children sit in a circle. If they agree with the statement you read out, they should stand up and change places. Once they have moved, you can ask their reason for moving or staying, and then supply the correct answer (if there is one). With a larger group this activity can be modified to become 'Stay standing if…' You may wish to add your own statements to this list.

💬 Stand and change places if:

You think it's possible for a person to hold their breath for 8 minutes.
True.

You think it's possible for a person to pull an aeroplane.
David Huxley pulled a Boeing 747–400, weighing 187 tonnes, a distance of 9 metres in 1 minute and 27.7 seconds on 15 October 1997 in Sydney, Australia.

You think it's possible for a person to balance a car on their head.
It's death defying, it's daunting and it's downright dangerous! But John Evans from Derbyshire, England balanced a 159.6kg Mini on his head for 33 seconds.

You think it's possible to live to be 122 years old.
Jeanne-Louise Calment, a French woman, lived for 122 years and 164 days. She was born in France on 21 February 1875. She was 14 when the Eiffel Tower was completed in 1889. She led an extremely active life, taking up fencing at 85 years old, and was still riding a bicycle at 100. She portrayed herself at the age of 114 in the film *Vincent and Me*, to become the oldest actress in film.

You think it's possible to travel at over 100km/h on a skateboard.
Gary Hardwick of Carlsbad, California, USA, set a skateboard speed record (maintaining a standing position) of 100.66km/h at Fountain Hills, Arizona, USA, on 26 September 1998. Gary had been boarding at speed for years and says he's been lucky to escape serious injury. However, he takes care to wear lots of safety gear such as leather clothing, helmet and gloves. He reckons the key to record speeds lies in aerodynamics.

Until 1954 athletes believed that no one could run a mile in under four minutes. That year, Roger Bannister achieved this and so challenged everyone's limiting belief in the four-minute barrier. Later that year several other athletes broke Bannister's record because they knew it was possible.

Our own performance is influenced by what we believe is possible. Do you hold limiting self-beliefs about what you can and can't do?

Workshop

What I believe affects what I feel, affects how I act and affects what I learn.

Activity 7: **What's your inner voice saying?**

Aim:	To start the thought process by which we can challenge limiting self-beliefs.
Resources:	Cards with challenging questions for each pair of children (pages 119–123).
Time:	10 minutes.

This can lead into a pair-work activity; however, it is best if the process is modelled by the tutor first. You will need another adult helper or one of the children to be the challenger.

Person A makes a statement about something they believe they cannot do. Person B responds by asking any of the challenging questions, which Person A must try to answer. For example:

> **Person A**: 'I'll never be able to get fit.'
>
> **Person B**: 'Who says you can't do it?'

Once Person A has answered Person B's question, they then move on to another statement about something they believe they cannot do. After about a minute the two swap roles.

Other challenging questions include:

- What would you need to make it possible?

- How would you feel if you could?

- Can you imagine yourself doing it?

- Imagine, what else could you do if you succeeded?

We limit what we are able to do by our own beliefs about ourselves. Remember Henry Ford's quote 'Whether you think you can or you think you can't – you're right.' If we believe we can, then we probably will. Roger Bannister believed he could run a mile in four minutes; very few others believed he could, but he did.

🗩 Are there any limiting beliefs we hold about our learning in general; our reading, writing, spelling, counting, multiplying, and so on?

Workshop

Quitters never win. Winners never quit!

1

Activity 8: **Cliff Young's story**

Aim:	To use the power of narrative to illustrate how one man surprised others.
Resources:	Copies of the story for the children to take home (pages 124–125).
Time:	10 minutes.

This activity looks at an example of how amazing positive thinking can be. The following summary of Cliff Young's story can be read to the class in order to get the children thinking about positive thinking and to stimulate group discussion:

💬 Cliff Young was 61 years old when he decided to enter one of the longest, most physically challenging marathons in the world. The Sydney to Melbourne race is around 600km long and takes about five days. A sheep farmer all his life with no racing experience, he had no idea how long the marathon would take. He simply went for it. He was competing with some of the world's fittest athletes, but took first place – nine hours ahead of the second place runner!

How did Cliff manage to win? He wasn't an athlet~~... he had no formal ...~~ent, he had no marathon training. Talk in groups and come up ~~with some of the qualities~~ Cliff must have had. What sort of person was he?

The main point here is that because Cliff hadn't ~~...~~ athlete, he had no preconceived ideas about it, no beliefs abou~~t ...~~

Remember: 'Whether you think you can or you think you ~~can't, you're right.'~~ ~~(Henry~~ Ford)

Cliff thought he could do it; everyone else thought he was ~~...~~ he let what other people thought stop him? He had a positive mental attitude; his past ~~exp~~erience on the farm made him think he could, he believed he could and he felt he could.

💬 What can we learn from Cliff?

💬 How might this help with your learning?

At the end of the session, you can give out copies of 'Cliff Young's story' for each child to take home, read and be inspired!

Workshop

'Never, never, never give up.'

Winston Churchill

U.F.A. Let's Learn How to Learn

Activity 9: **Agree or disagree?**

Aim:	To consolidate work done so far.
Resources:	Posters for the three stations (pages 126–128); plenty of space.
Time:	10 minutes.

This is a physical activity. The three stations representing 'Agree', 'Disagree' and 'Don't know' can be fixed in different parts of the room, or three volunteers could wear different coloured sports bibs indicating the contrasting viewpoints. If you choose to do it this way, the stations can move too.

The tutor makes a series of statements; after each one, everyone has to move to whichever station best describes their viewpoint. Statements can include:

- Your past experience can affect the way you feel about something.
- 'Whether you think you can or you think you can't – you're right.' (Henry Ford).
- A positive state of mind is more important than intelligence.
- I can do anything.
- Your beliefs can be limiting.
- Cliff Young was just lucky.
- Smiling and laughing helps you feel more positive.
- How you feel about something will affect whether you can achieve it.
- You are what you think.

Add other statements of your choice.

Break for discussion at any interesting points or suggest that the children ask each other, 'Why do you think that?' when they have moved to a station.

◼ *Points to make* ▬▬▬▬▬▶

✓ People are motivated by their interests: being interested in something makes you want to do it more.

✓ People are motivated by feeling confident: when you feel confident about something, you don't mind having a go.

✓ People are motivated by what they think is important: if you think something is important, you will put more effort into it.

✓ People are sometimes motivated by other people's threats or promises: sometimes you want to do something to prove other people wrong when they think you can't do it, or because there's a prize or reward if you succeed.

Workshop

You haven't lost until you stop trying!

Activity 10: **Challenging my thoughts**

Aim:	To encourage children to challenge any limiting self-belief about schoolwork by thinking about their motivation to do it.
Resources:	Copies of the 'Challenging my thoughts' resource sheet (page 129). You will need at least two copies per child.
Time:	20 minutes.

🗨 OK. We're now going to think about your schoolwork. Think about something that you're good at (sums, science, story writing, spelling) or something that is important to you.

Using the 'Challenging my thoughts!' sheet, draw a picture of yourself or write your name in the box. Colour in the statements or thoughts that come into your mind when you think about the type of work you've chosen. You can colour in as many or as few statements as you wish. You can also capture any other thoughts on the back of the page.

● What do you notice about your thoughts when you think of something you like?

● How many positive thoughts are there compared to negative ones?

● Do you think this makes you like or enjoy that activity more?

● Do you think this affects how good you are at the activity? Why?

Now, using the other copy, repeat the process, thinking about something you are not so good at or don't like.

Now ask the same questions about an activity you are less enthusiastic about.

You'd probably agree with the following statements. When thinking of something you are good at, enjoy or which is important to you:

● When asked to do that thing, it's no problem.

● You don't really mind spending time doing it.

OK. Now think about something that you think is pointless, or something that you think you can't do.

● The chances are this is something you will avoid doing.

● You'll be easily distracted when doing it.

● You'll generally not do it well.

Workshop

Today is a great day to learn something new.

U.F.A. Let's Learn How to Learn

■ Activity 10: **Challenging my thoughts** (continued)

💬 Your brain/mind will believe what you tell it. If you tell it you are no good at something, it will act in that way. At the first difficulty you may decide that, well, you're no good at it so you won't carry on. This means that the next time you try to do this task you will remember that you failed the last time, and carry on feeling you are no good at it. Therefore, how you feel affects how you act, which affects how you feel. You can become trapped by your thoughts. But you can break this cycle if you want to. If you tell your brain the opposite – that you can do something – you are more likely to carry on until you succeed because you believe you are capable of succeeding.

Let's go back and think about what you find hard, feel you can't do well or feel is pointless. It might be reading, doing sums, science or learning spellings.

In order to get yourself motivated try to:

● think, 'Why do I want to do this?'

● think long term: 'What will it help me to do?'

● listen to what your inner voice is saying. When you think about it, are you really saying, 'I **can't**' or 'I **won't**'? Think about the challenging questions we used in Activity 7 – how can you challenge your own inner voice about this thing?

If you think carefully about why you need to do this thing, you'll probably come up with a good reason. Once you have, you'll be much more likely to have a positive mental attitude towards it.

Make a promise to yourself that you are going to change what your inner voice is saying about this. Make sure you tell someone what it is that you're going to try to change – perhaps tell a friend, your teacher or someone at home.

Variations

You may feel that the children would benefit from exploring negative or positive thoughts prior to colouring in the sheets. Indeed, some of the statements are open to interpretation, and discussion may be useful to broaden perceptions of certain thoughts. You could put each of the statements from the sheet on to card and cut them up. The children could then sort them into piles of 'negative' or 'positive' statements, and talk about why they came to the decisions they did.

Workshop

U.F.A. Let's Learn How to Learn

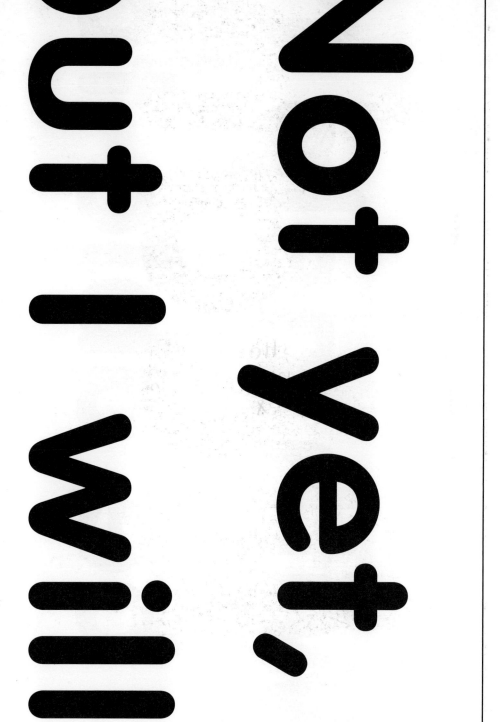

Not yet, but I will

Activity 4

With help I'll be able to

kind	friendly
helpful	funny
thoughtful	considerate
polite	gentle
hard working	reflective

Activity 5

warm	witty
confident	imaginative
enthusiastic	creative
lively	generous
determined	precise

U.F.A. Let's Learn How to Learn

reliable	keen
understanding	careful
respectful	co-operative

Activity 5

This is me

name:

Activity 5

Who says you can't do it?

Activity 7

What would you need to make it possible?

How would you feel if you could?

Activity 7

Can you imagine yourself doing it?

Imagine, what else could you do if you succeeded?

Activity 7

Cliff Young's story

Every year, Australia hosts a 600km race from Sydney to Melbourne. It's a long, tough race that makes other marathons look easy. It takes five days.

In 1983, a guy named Cliff Young showed up to run in the race. Nobody knew he was planning to run because he was 61 years old, and showed up in overalls and galoshes over his work boots to join a group of 150 world-class athletes.

This is a big race – we're talking about Nike sponsorship and fit young men and women who run these endurance races all over the world.

As Cliff walked up to the table to take his number, it became clear to everybody that he was going to run. They all thought, 'This must be a publicity stunt. Who's backing this guy? He'll drop out in 30 minutes. He's 61 years old. He's wearing rubber galoshes and overalls. This is crazy!'

But the press were curious, so as he took his number and moved into the pack of runners, all wearing their special, expensive racing gear, the media moved their microphones into Cliff's face and asked, 'Who are you and what are you doing?'

'I'm Cliff Young. I'm from a large ranch outside of Melbourne, where we keep sheep.'

They said, 'You're really going to run in this race?'

'Yeah,' Cliff nodded.

'Got any backers?'

'No.'

'Then you can't run.'

'Yeah I can.' Cliff replied. 'See, I grew up on a farm where we couldn't afford horses or four-wheel drives, and the whole time I was growing up – until about four years ago when we finally made some money and got a four-wheeler – whenever the storms would roll in, I'd have to go out and round up the sheep. We had 2,000 sheep, and we have 2,000 acres. Sometimes I would have to run round those sheep for two or three days. It took a long time, but I'd catch them. I believe I can run this race. It's only two more days – five days. I've run sheep for three.'

When Cliff Young started the race alongside all the world-class athletes, people shouted, 'Somebody stop him, he'll die! He's crazy!' They broadcast it on the news immediately, so all of Australia was watching this crazy guy shuffling along in his galoshes.

The way most people ran the race was to run for 18 hours and then sleep for six. But Cliff didn't stop after the first 18 hours. He kept running. Every night he got just a little bit closer to the rest. By the last night, he passed them. By the last day, he was way in front of them. Not only did he run the Sydney to Melbourne race at age 61 – all 600km, without dying – he came first by nine hours and became a national hero!

When he finished the race, the media asked him what he thought enabled him to win. Cliff didn't know you were supposed to sleep! His experience was chasing sheep, trying to outrun a storm – with no time to sleep.

Cliff Young, with every conceivable limitation against him, changed the whole way that race was run. Now, nobody sleeps. To win the race, you have to run all night as well as all day. And you know what's really funny? Many recent winners of the race over the last few years, have run using the 'Young shuffle', because it's more aerodynamic than the way the world-class runners were running before!

Activity 8

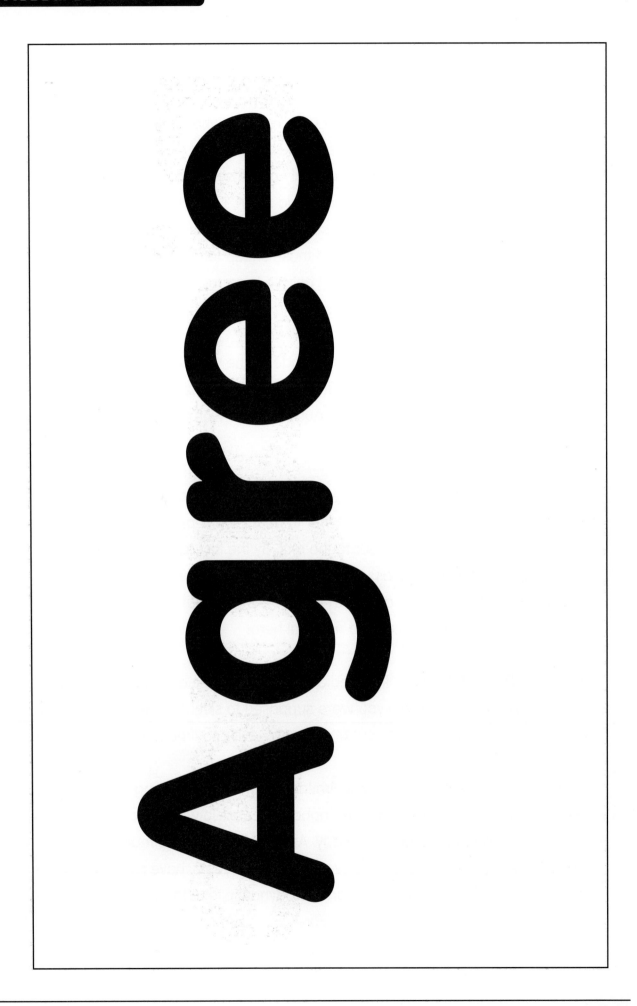

Agree

Activity 9

U.F.A. Let's Learn How to Learn

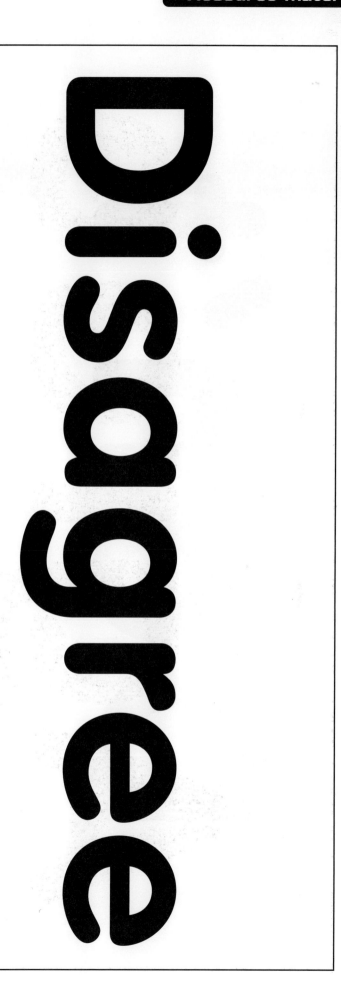

Disagree

Activity 9

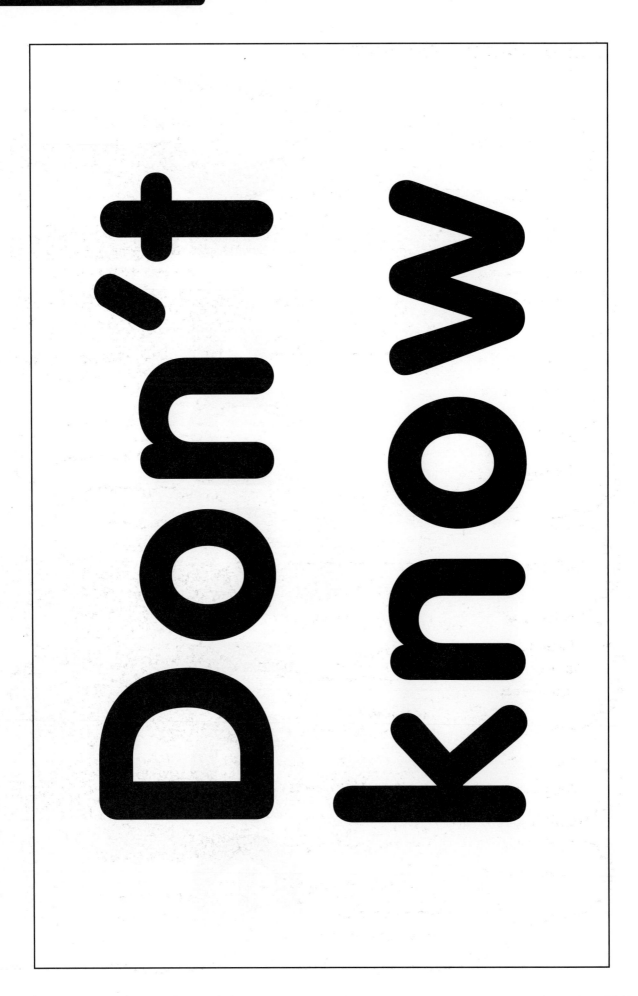

Don't know

Challenging my thoughts!

Great!

That's okay.

Sounds hard.

I can do it!

Why *do* I have to do this?

I'm scared.

I'm sure I could do this if I get some help.

Looking forward to this.

Oh no!

I hate this sort of thing.

I can't do this.

Excellent!

Boring.

Sounds easy.

name:..........................

I'm no good at this.

I will enjoy this.

I am going to need help with this.

Interesting.

I really love doing this.

Not looking forward to this.

I don't want to do it.

I know who can help me.

I'm good at this.

Last time, I got it right.

I am going to have fun.

I don't care.

I know someone who can already do this.

Last time, I got it wrong.

'Wonderful, bizarre, wicked, weird, very creative.'

UFA student

U.F.A. Let's Learn How to Learn

Learning in different ways

We are as individual as our faces and fingerprints.

U.F.A. Let's Learn How to Learn

Introduction

Our brains make sense of the outside world through all of our five senses. The field of Neuro-Linguistic Programming suggests that we re-create and make sense of that information in three ways – **visual**, **auditory** and **kinesthetic** (VAK) – and we may have a preference for how we do this. It suggests that, for us to learn most effectively, we need to have information presented to us in a way that matches our preferred 'learning style'. Children and young people will be able to learn more effectively if they are aware of how they learn and understand that effective learning engages all of their senses.

By helping children to understand how they learn, we can support them in valuing differences, legitimizing their approach to learning. They are then free to develop a range of strategies that support their learning journey, and prevent the negativity that can arise when some children see themselves as failures. It is also important to remember that everyone develops at their own pace.

In her book, *The Power of Diversity* (2004), Barbara Prashnig's model of learning styles includes VAK, but splits kinesthetic into kinesthetic and tactile. She also suggests a developmental cycle which builds upon these senses. The first modalities to develop are our kinesthetic and tactile ones, and this is why young children need to touch so much; they learn through manipulation and interaction with objects and people. Most very young children begin experiencing the world and learning kinesthetically; their whole body is involved and only later will they begin to access their learning primarily through visual or auditory modes. Our visual modality develops when we are about eight years old, when we begin to develop a strong preference for taking in information through observation and watching. Children tend to become more able to access learning through auditory stimulus from about 11 years of age. The majority of learners remain highly kinesthetic and tactile during their primary years; only a few are strongly visual or auditory. Prashnig's research has revealed that even gifted and highly talented adolescents remain strongly tactile and kinesthetic.

Specifically, both children and adults demonstrate these modalities in three different ways. The following concepts are drawn from Alistair Smith's work, and for further reference, consult *Accelerated Learning in Practice*, page 145.

If you have a *visual* preference, then you will find it easy to build up mental pictures. You readily 'see' yourself operating in different contexts. You'll see images associated with words or feelings, and they will affirm your understanding of new information only when you see it happen or see it written or described visually. When spelling, you may 'see' the word as you are about to write it out.

If you have an *auditory* preference, it is expressed through a preference for internal dialogue and through language generally. You may 'hear' the word spelled out before writing it. In anticipating a new situation, you may have a mental rehearsal of what will be said by and to you.

With a *kinesthetic* preference, you will often use strong emotional attachments. In spelling a word you may feel yourself writing it letter by letter beforehand or it may simply feel right.

The activities in this workshop encourage children to explore their current personal preferences and to build a range of different approaches that can be used in a variety of situations. This self-awareness of preferred learning styles is not about labelling ourselves or others as a particular type of learner, but rather seeing the breadth of approaches that are possible. It is likely that using all the senses secures the learning far more deeply than a more narrow approach.

Family challenge

I've been finding out how my senses help me to learn.

Help me find out about you as a learner by filling in the questionnaire. I'll help you and explain what it means.

Everybody is different and learns in different ways.

Take it home – let's learn together!

Part 1: **Workshop plan**

By the end of this workshop children will:

- understand more about how their senses contribute to their learning
- have found out more about themselves as individual learners
- have begun to think about how different strategies can be used in different learning situations.

The big idea
We all learn in different ways.

Activity 1: **Would you rather?**
(warm-up activity -- 10–12 minutes)

Activity 2: **Discovering more about me as a learner**
(20 minutes)

Activity 3: **Different strategies for different learners**
(20 minutes)

Activity 4: **Introducing myself as a learner**
(20 minutes)

Family challenge
Take it home – let's learn together!

! *Don't forget to experiment with brain breaks (see page 13) – either at the start of the session or after about 20 minutes.*

❛To learn anything fast and effectively you have to see it, hear it, feel it.❜

Tony Stockwell

U.F.A. Let's Learn How to Learn

Activity 1: **Would you rather?**

Aim:	To raise awareness that we are all different and like to do things in different ways.
Resources:	None.
Time:	10–12 minutes.

Label the two sides of the room 'A' and 'B'. Pupils have to run to the appropriate side in response to the questions below. Remind the children that they must make a decision, and cannot choose both!

Would you rather:

A		B
eat chocolate ice cream	or	strawberry ice cream?
stay up late	or	go to bed early?
watch a film	or	read a book?
work by yourself	or	work with others?
draw a picture	or	write a story?
work in a noisy room	or	work in a quiet room?
read a book yourself	or	listen to a story?
learn something new by yourself	or	learn something new with other people?
use a dictionary to find a spelling	or	ask someone a spelling?

Add other questions of your choice.

Points to make

✓ We have preferences for how we do things and what we like. They are not right or wrong; it's just that everyone is different.

✓ Knowing how you prefer to do things will help you to make the most of your learning opportunities.

Workshop

❝Emblazon these words on your mind … learning is most effective when it's fun.❞

Peter Kline

The Everyday Genius: Restoring Children's Natural Joy of Learning and Yours Too,
© 1988, Great River Books, Inc., Salt Lake City, Utah.

Activity 2: **Discovering more about me as a learner**

Aims:	● To raise awareness of what children are like as individual learners and to discover the things that help them learn or hinder their learning.
	● To realize that everyone has a different way of learning and that each way is equally valid.
Resources:	Copies of the VAK questionnaire: either text (pages 155–156) or mind map version (page 157); VAK posters (pages 158–160).
Time:	20 minutes.

Different people like information to be presented in different ways. Some people like to see it, some like to read it, some may be happy to have someone explain it, while others prefer to actually do something with it before they feel they understand it.

The VAK questionnaire will help us to work out how we prefer to learn at the moment. As we get older we learn to use all our senses to take in information.

Put the supporting VAK posters supplied in three separate areas of the room. These posters comprise: visual (an eye), auditory (an ear) and kinesthetic (a hand). Ask the children to complete the VAK questionnaire. This can be done individually or you may prefer to read each statement out to the group and ask them to record their responses. When the children have finished the questionnaire and worked out their learning preference, they can move to the area of the room where the specific poster represents their preferred learning style.

The VAK mind map questionnaire is an alternative questionnaire that the students can colour in. This format gives them the bigger picture of their learning styles because they are able to see that they use elements of all the styles, although one may be more dominant. This mind map could be filled in additionally or as an alternative to the VAK questionnaire, or could be used as a review activity.

▰▰ *Points to make* ▰▰▰▰▰▰▰▰▰▰▰▶

✓ This information gives the children new ways of approaching their learning.

✓ If the children are given information in a way that doesn't suit their preference, they will now be able to take control of their learning and make it work for them.

✓ Learning is most successful when we can work with all of our different senses, so the children will need to practise and experience all the different ways of taking in information.

✓ The children can use different approaches for different contexts. They have choices about the approaches they have at their disposal.

Workshop

We take in information by:

Seeing (visual)

Hearing (auditory)

Doing (kinesthetic)

However, the best way to learn is through all of our senses at the same time.

This is

multisensory learning.

Activity 3: **Different strategies for different learners**

Aim:	To raise awareness of the range of strategies that can be used to achieve the same outcome and realize that some strategies are more suitable for some contexts than others.
Resources:	None.
Time:	20 minutes.

Divide the children into small groups and ask each group to focus on one approach to learning spellings (either V, A or K).

Some example words are noted below for this activity, but you may wish to substitute your own words.

💬 As a visual (or auditory or kinesthetic) learner, how many different ways (or strategies) can you come up with for learning these spellings:

receive   because   separate   necessary   another

There are three parts to this activity:

First of all, I'd like you to brainstorm and collect all your ideas as a group.

Then, once you have all your ideas together, divide them into two categories: strategies that can be used on their own, and strategies that need other people to work with. You could colour code your ideas or rewrite them in two lists.

Finally, we're going to display your ideas on the wall for the other groups to look at.

The children can then have a few minutes to look at the work of the other groups, or you could ask each group to share their top two or three ideas with the rest of the class.

◼️▤ *Points to make* ▰▰▰▰▰▰▰▰▰▰▰▰▶

✓ Even though we may have a preference for one particular style of learning, we should aim to use all the different styles. Seeing things in different ways helps to keep us challenged and stops us from getting bored (boredom stops us from remembering and learning).

✓ Knowing and using a greater range of strategies gives us more choices; when one method doesn't work, we can try another rather than give up.

Workshop

Everyone is intelligent.

U.F.A. Let's Learn How to Learn

Activity 4: **Introducing myself as a learner**

Aim:	To give children a chance to reflect and capture all they have found out about themselves. The end product can be shared with other teachers and parents to inform them, too.
Resources:	A photograph of each child. Either ask the children to bring in a recent photograph of themselves or use a digital camera to take a snapshot of each child. Some students may want to use the writing frame, 'All about me as a Super Learner!' (page 161).
Time:	20 minutes.

In this review activity the class can compile a 'Who's Who?' booklet or a display for the group. Explain that everyone will have a page in the book, to introduce themselves as a learner.

💬 This page will include a photograph (or drawing) of yourself and the following information:

● what you like doing

● how you like to learn

● how you remember things

● what makes learning hard for you

● two or three strategies you like using to remember spellings.

Children can choose to draw a mind map, use the writing frame or create their own way of sharing this information.

You may want to extend this activity and ask each child to introduce their partner to the group, using what they have created.

◼️ *Points to make*

✓ Everyone is different and likes to do things in different ways. No one way is better or worse than any other.

✓ It's OK to be you!

Workshop

Family challenge

I'm going to talk to at least three different people.

I've been finding out how my senses can help me to learn my spellings.

Tell me how you learn new spellings, and I'll tell you three new ways you could try.

Take it home – let's learn together!

U.F.A. Let's Learn How to Learn

Part 2: **Workshop plan**

By the end of this workshop children will:

- understand more about their preferred learning styles

- have experienced a range of strategies and understand how and when to use them.

The big idea
We need to try out as many different ways of learning as possible.

Activity 5: **Find someone who ...**
(10 minutes)

Activity 6: **VAK spelling circus**
(45 minutes)

Activity 7: **So what have I learned?**
(15 minutes)

Family challenge
Take it home – let's learn together!

Don't forget to experiment with brain breaks (see page 13) – either at the start of the session or after about 20 minutes.

Visual learning

- 👁 Make a mind map.

- 👁 Draw pictures to show the learning.

- 👁 Use diagrams and graphs.

- 👁 Colour code the learning.

Activity 5: **Find someone who ...**

Aim:	To remind the children that everyone is different and that there are many ways of learning. It is also a kinesthetic activity that gets them up and moving, talking to one another and valuing differences.
Resources:	A copy of the 'Find someone who ...' activity sheet (page 162) for each child.
Time:	10 minutes.

This warm-up exercise encourages children to walk around the room and talk to as many different people as possible about the different things written on their balloon tags.

When they find someone who relates to what's written on a balloon tag, they can write that person's name in the balloon (or invite them to write their own name in the balloon).

◀▌▐ *Points to make* ▬▬▬▬▬▬▬▬▬▬▬▬▬▬▬▶

✓ Knowing about how classmates like to learn can be very useful, too. You may sometimes want to work with other people to get and give help. Everyone has their own way of learning.

Workshop

Auditory learning

🦻 Say it out loud.

🦻 Tell someone else about it.

🦻 Use a tape recorder.

🦻 Put the learning to music.

🦻 Use rhymes and rhythms.

U.F.A. Let's Learn How to Learn

Activity 6: **VAK spelling circus**

Aim:	For the children to experience and so raise their awareness of a range of learning strategies to help them learn spellings.
Resources:	Copies of all three VAK 'strategies for spelling' sheets (pages 163–165); copies of all three VAK lists of spelling words (pages 166–168); copies of the visual spelling posters for each child to colour in (pages 169–173) – enough for each child at the relevant workstations. You will also need specific resources for each workstation (see below).
Time:	45 minutes.

Set up the 'V', 'A' and 'K' workstations with all the relevant resource sheets, so that there are enough for each child to pick up and work on as they move round the VAK spelling circus, along with a selection of sense-specific resources, as listed below.

Divide the students into three groups. These don't have to reflect learning styles; in fact, they would be more effective if each group contained a variety of learning styles.

Each group begins at one of three workstations: visual, auditory or kinesthetic.

At each workstation, the students have 15 minutes to learn the spellings of five words, using the strategies suggested. They are given a range of methods and can choose which one they want to work with.

Visual

Spellings: passenger   encounter   climbing   gleaming   together

Resources:

- sheets of plain and lined paper (various sizes and colours)
- plenty of coloured felt-tip pens and highlighters
- post-it notes
- copies of the words that can be coloured in
- copies of strategies to use and take away.

Kinesthetic learning

🖐 Learn with your body.

🖐 Make your learning active.

🖐 Move around.

🖐 Use actions and mimes.

U.F.A. Let's Learn How to Learn

■ Activity 6: **VAK spelling circus** *(continued)*

Auditory

Spellings: among   pollution   actually   serious   know

Resources:

- sheets of lined paper, pens and pencils
- mirror for students to look into as they make the sounds of words
- tape recorder and tape of the target words for students to listen to
- another tape recorder with a blank tape and a microphone for students to record themselves spelling the words out loud, and listen back to the recording
- some simple musical instruments, for example, drum, maracas
- copies of strategies to use and take away.

Kinesthetic

Spellings: believe   actually   pollution   surprise   pierce

Resources:

- pieces of blank card about 5cm x 5cm square
- post-it notes
- felt-tip pens
- resources for children to make the words, such as plasticine, fridge letter magnets, fuzzy felt, glitter and glue, and so on.
- copies of strategies to use and take away.

You will notice that the words 'pollution' and 'actually' appear in two different workstations. Ask the children if they found it easier to remember these spellings better because they've learned them in different ways.

At the end of this activity, you may like to take a few minutes to discuss the children's findings, and the effectiveness of learning through all of our senses.

◼◼ *Points to make*

✓ It is useful to know a range of strategies for learning using all of the senses, not just your preferred one. When one way doesn't fully work, you should try another and not just give up.

✓ Although this activity has focused on spelling, some of the strategies can be used for any type of learning.

Workshop

Multisensory spelling

Write the words in lots of different ways:

- Write the word in the air.

- Write the word in CAPITALS, in lower case and in joined-up writing.

- Write the word on a rough surface with your finger.

- Say the word out loud – hear the word.

- Write the word on your arm with your finger – feel the word.

- Write the word in different colours.

- Repeat the spelling of the word over and over again.

- Put coloured circles round parts of the word you specially need to remember.

- Write the word as individual letters and then rearrange them – feel the word.

Can you think of any other ways of writing the words?

Activity 7: **So what have I learned?**

Aim:	To give the children time to reflect on the various strategies they have tried, and capture the ones that have had most impact so that they can use them again.
Resources:	None.
Time:	15 minutes.

Ask the children which two strategies they have learned today they are confident that they can use on their own when learning new spellings, both:

● at home and

● at school.

Ask them to find a partner so they can share their ideas.

Points to make

✓ When thinking about which strategy to use, you need to think about where you are, who you are with and what resources you have.

✓ It is worth trying out all the strategies a number of times before you decide which work best for you.

✓ Having a range of strategies to choose from means that you are a more adaptable, flexible learner.

Variations

This could form the basis for a more in-depth piece of work for children to do some individual goal-setting and action-planning.

Workshop

Enjoy learning. Learning is fun!

U.F.A. Let's Learn How to Learn

VAK questionnaire

Tick the box that describes you best.

1 When you think about spelling a word, do you:

See the word?   ☐ V

Sound the word out?   ☐ A

Write the word down to see if it looks right?   ☐ K

2 When you are really concentrating, are you distracted by:

Messiness and untidiness?   ☐ V

Noise, talking and music?   ☐ A

Movement?   ☐ K

3 When you remember special events, do you recall them with:

Pictures and images?   ☐ V

Sounds?   ☐ A

Moving pictures?   ☐ K

4 When you are angry, do you:

Stay silent, but remain really angry inside?   ☐ V

Shout loudly?   ☐ A

Clench your fists, grit your teeth and stamp about?   ☐ K

5 When you forget an incident that has happened or a person you've met, do you:

Forget names but remember faces?   ☐ V

Forget faces but remember names?   ☐ A

Remember only where you were and what you did?   ☐ K

6 When describing an object, for example, your front door, would you:

See it in your mind?   ☐ V

Describe it with words?   ☐ A

Think how it feels, sounds or opens, and so on?   ☐ K

Activity 2

Resource material

7 When you are learning, do you prefer:

Work that is written down in many colours?   ☐ V

Listening to a person talk or give instructions?   ☐ A

Take part in making or doing activities?   ☐ K

8 In your spare time, do you prefer to:

Watch TV, read or play computer games?   ☐ V

Listen to music?   ☐ A

Play sports and games?   ☐ K

9 When you are talking, do you:

Talk little and don't want to listen for too long?   ☐ V

Like to listen and talk as well?   ☐ A

Talk with your hands and gesture a lot?   ☐ K

10 When you receive praise or a reward, do you prefer to:

Receive a written note or certificate?   ☐ V

Hear it said to you?   ☐ A

Be given a 'pat on the back' or a handshake?   ☐ K

Total number of Vs (visual) 👁   ☐

Total number of As (auditory) 👂   ☐

Total number of Ks (kinesthetic) ✋   ☐

The letter with the highest score indicates your preferred way of learning.

Many people do not have a really strong preference and can work easily with all three styles. If you have roughly equal scores, this may be you!

Your preferred way of learning may be different at different times for different tasks, and may change as you get older.

Activity 2

U.F.A. Let's Learn How to Learn

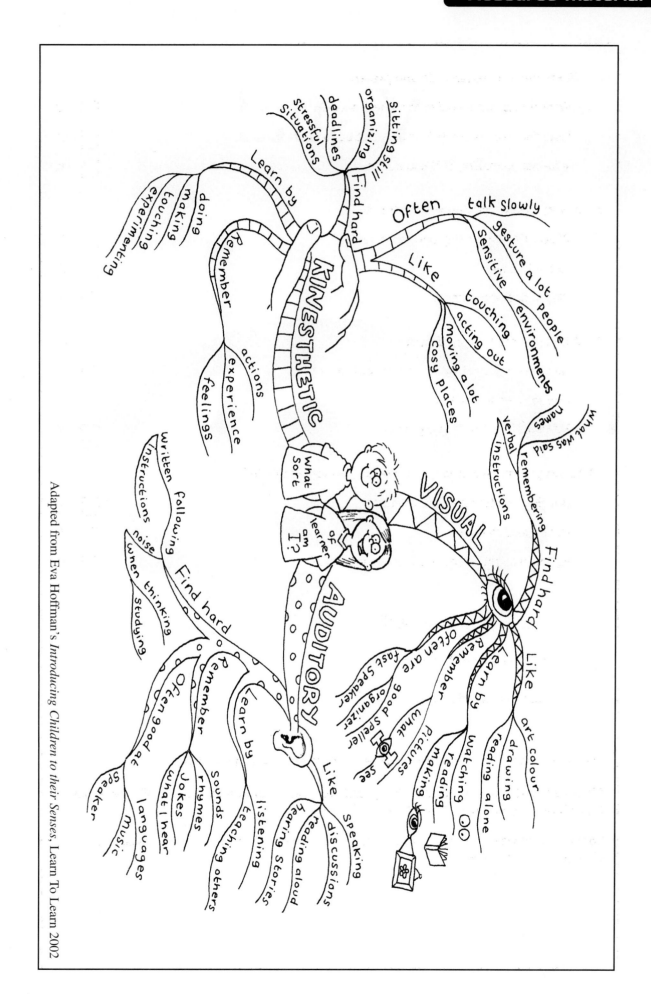

Adapted from Eva Hoffman's *Introducing Children to their Senses*, Learn To Learn 2002

Visual

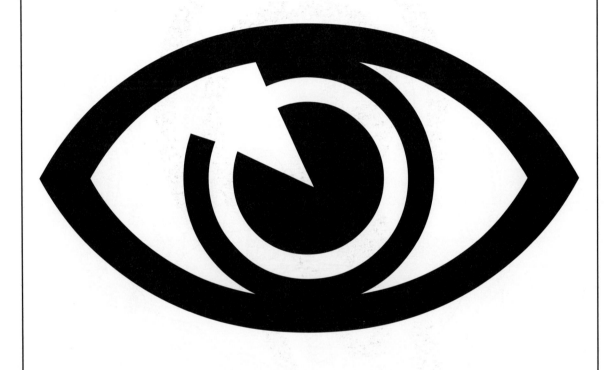

Auditory

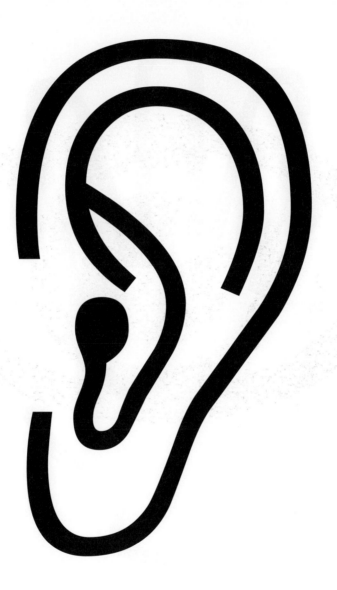

Kinesthetic

All about me as a Super Learner!

Name: ....

Things I enjoy doing are:

1 ....
2 ....
3 ....

I like to learn by ....

and ....

I remember things easily when I ....

....

I find learning hard when:

1 ....
2 ....
3 ....

Three ways I like to learn spellings:

1 ....
2 ....
3 ....

Activity 4

Find someone who...

enjoys listening and talking things over with other people.

can tell you how they like to learn.

can tell you two ways they use to remember things.

likes to move about when they are learning.

gets annoyed if there is music playing while they are working.

would prefer to watch a film rather than read a book.

enjoys doodling.

Activity 5

U.F.A. Let's Learn How to Learn

Visual strategies for spelling

Use some of the following strategies to learn the spellings you have been given.

- 👁 Use a highlighter to highlight any hidden words in your main word.

- 👁 Colour in the word, adding any pictures/symbols to each of the letters to help you remember them.

- 👁 Imagine the letters of the word in your mind. Make them unusual in some way.

- 👁 Colour code the spellings you are learning. Use colours to pick out patterns in the way the words are spelled.

- 👁 Write out the word as many times as you can. Look carefully at it and notice any patterns. Make silent letters stand out, using colour, symbols or pictures.

- 👁 Write the spellings in different colours and display them around the room. Put them at eye height, so they can be easily seen.

- 👁 Design a poster for each spelling, using pictures and lots of colour.

Activity 6

Auditory strategies for spelling

You may either read the spellings you have been given, or listen to them on tape. Try some of the following strategies to help you learn the spellings.

- With a partner read the words aloud, paying close attention to the way they sound. Now try reading the words to yourself 'under your breath'. Try exaggerating the sounds.

- Say the words, breaking them up into chunks or syllables.

- Say the words, sounding out the silent letters too.

- Spell out the words, using the names – not sounds – of the letters.

- Experiment with different ways of saying the words out loud (emphasize different parts of the word, use different voices).

- Make up a sentence (mnemonic) using each letter of the word to remember the spelling, for example, 'because': **B**ig **E**lephants **C**annot **A**lways **U**se **S**mall **E**ntrances.

- Use musical instruments to add rhythm or sound to the spelling of the word.

- Make up a rhyme, rap, song or tune to the spelling.

- Listen to a tape of the target words and their spellings.

- Tape yourself spelling out the word, then listen to it to check you have the correct spelling.

- Sing the spelling.

- Look at yourself in the mirror while you make the sounds and spellings of the words.

- In pairs, test each other aloud.

Activity 6

UFA. Let's Learn How to Learn

Kinesthetic strategies for spelling

Try a few of the following strategies to revise the information you have been given.

- Go for a walk or move around as you say the spellings out loud.

- Write out the letters of each spelling on pieces of card, shuffle them up and put them back in order.

- Using post-it notes, write down each of the spellings. Assemble the notes on the wall, grouping any similar patterns together. How many different ways of grouping the words can you find?

- With your group spell out the word, using your bodies or any other resources provided to make the letters.

- Spell out the word, writing it in the air with your hand. As you do this, say the letters out loud.

- Count the number of letters in each word. Then hold up that number of fingers as you spell out the word. This will help you check you have included the right number of letters in your spelling.

- Working in pairs, take it in turns to write the spelling of the word on your partner's back. Your partner has to guess what word you have written.

Use a range of **visual** strategies for learning the following spellings:

passenger

encounter

climbing

gleaming

together

Use a range of **auditory** strategies for learning the following spellings:

among

pollution

actually

serious

know

Activity 6

Use a range of **kinesthetic** strategies for learning the following spellings:

believe

actually

pollution

surprise

pierce

U.F.A. Let's Learn How to Learn

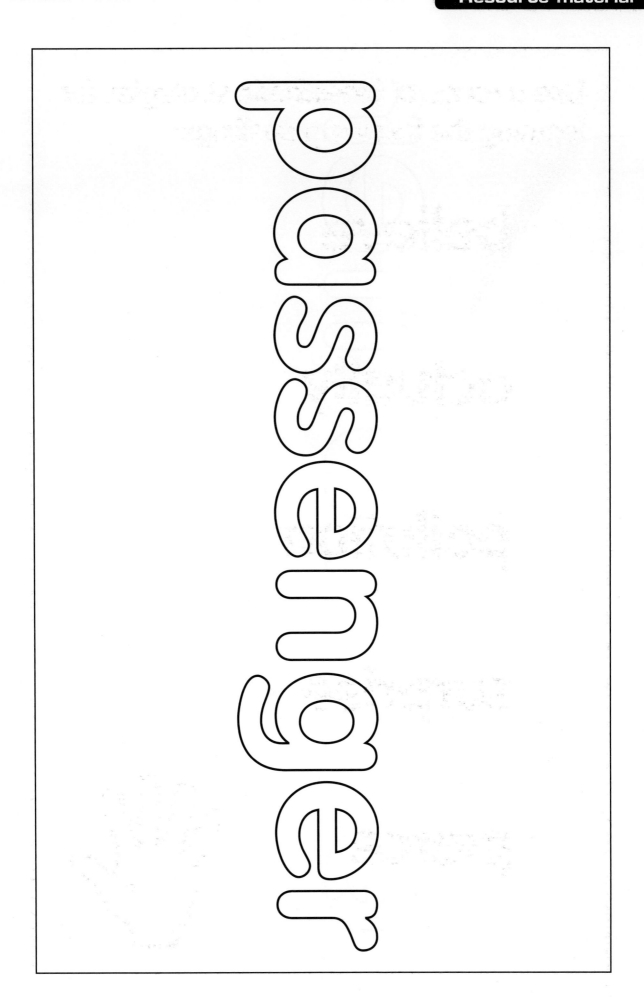

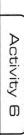

Activity 6

Activity 6

Activity 6

Activity 6

'I was learning and having fun at the same time.'

UFA student

U.F.A. Let's Learn How to Learn

My mega memory!

'It didn't feel like work!'

UFA student

U.F.A. Let's Learn How to Learn

Introduction

Memory is complex, and we don't yet fully understand how it works. It is likely that we use different memory systems in different situations, so remembering how to ride a bike uses a very different kind of memory system to the one used for remembering facts and figures. What we do know is that our current assessment methods require children to recall from memory what they have learned. We also know that we can help them improve this recall by understanding more about how we remember and by teaching memory techniques.

Linking and association are really important concepts to get across, and the activities in this workshop aim to present them in easy-to-understand ways. If children understand how their memories work, they will then be able to make active decisions about how they try to remember things. The workshop also aims to show how some things are naturally memorable. It then moves on to explore how we can make other things that we want to remember more memorable by applying some tried and tested strategies to them. By the end of Part 2 the children will have created their own memory tool.

Many of the techniques introduced here are well known and widely used – some are even used by world champions in memorization, who are able to perform amazing feats of memory!

Family challenge

I've been learning about how my memory works. Can I tell you?

We've been learning about how it is important to link things together to remember them. We played the tray game.

Can I try the 'Random letters brain teaser!' out on you?

Take it home – let's learn together!

U.F.A. Let's Learn How to Learn

Part 1: **Workshop plan**

By the end of this workshop children will have:

- explored the concept of memory and have a better understanding of how their memory works
- tried out some techniques for memorizing.

The big idea

We all have amazingly powerful memories – we just need to understand how to use them.

'The more you link the more you learn.'

Jeannette Vos, *The Learning Revolution*

Activity 1: **Remembering**
(5–10 minutes)

Activity 2: **Step forward if …**
(10 minutes)

Activity 3: **What's on the tray?**
(15 minutes)

Activity 4: **Making associations**
(5–10 minutes)

Activity 5: **Chunking to remember**
(15 minutes)

Activity 6: **Brain teaser! Random letters?**
(5 minutes)

Activity 7: **Remembering some more**
(5–10 minutes)

Family challenge
Take it home – let's learn together!

Don't forget to experiment with brain breaks (see page 13) – either at the start of the session or after about 20 minutes.

Help your memory by...

- Getting enough sleep (6–8 hours).

- Learning in chunks.

- Going over your learning again – and again.

- Making it important.

U.F.A. Let's Learn How to Learn

Activity 1: **Remembering**

Aim:	For children to begin to think about how memories work.
Resources:	None.
Time:	5–10 minutes.

Explain to the group that you will be asking them to remember certain things. It is important that everyone feels comfortable where they are, because for some of the remembering they may want to close their eyes.

💬 Can you remember:

- What you had for breakfast today?
- Your route to school each day?
- What your favourite song sounds like?
- What is on the wall next to your bed at home?
- Somewhere you went on holiday?
- One of your birthday presents you received this year?

How many of you were able to remember these things? Why did so many of us remember these things?

Some things are easy to remember, such as what we do every day, places or songs we know well, what has happened recently, occasions that stick out because they are special, like holidays and birthdays, or times when we have been very happy or very sad.

What does this tell us about our memories?

Points to make

- ✓ We remember things if they are special or different.
- ✓ We remember things that have happened recently.
- ✓ We remember things that we have done over and over again or do every day.
- ✓ We remember things if there are strong emotions linked to them.

Workshop

Don't forget...

70 per cent of what you learn is forgotten in 24 hours.

About 40 per cent is forgotten immediately!

You must review regularly!

U.F.A. Let's Learn How to Learn

Activity 2: **Step forward if ...**

Aim:	To get children thinking about memory.
Resources:	None (other than sufficient space for movement).
Time:	10 minutes.

This is a quick warm-up activity to get the children thinking and talking about memory. Ask the group to form a standing circle. Explain that you will be giving the group some statements and if any of them are true for them individually, or if they think they can answer them, they step forward. After you have read out a statement, you could ask some of the children to talk about why they stepped forward – or stayed put.

Before moving on to the next statement, ask everyone who has moved to step back to create a circle again.

Use some of the following statements and add your own if you like.

🗩 Step forward if ...

- You think your memory is useful.

- You can give an example of when you use your memory (in school or out of school).

- You think it is ever good to forget.

- You think you have a good memory.

- You can give the group one reason why you think it is important to have a good memory.

- You can explain what your memory is.

- You would like to improve your memory.

- You think your brain is like a sieve.

- You know how many different sorts of memory you have.

With the last statement, you could take the opportunity to talk about how scientists currently believe we have at least three types of memory: immediate, short term and long term. You could also mention that we remember different things in different ways – we may remember facts in one way, but use different methods to remember skills and things we do, for example, riding a bike, playing a musical instrument or kicking a football.

Workshop

'I remembered everything on the list!'

UFA student

U.F.A. Let's Learn How to Learn

Activity 3: **What's on the tray?**

Aim:	To show how our short-term memory is limited in the amount of information it can hold.
Resources:	15–20 everyday objects; tray; cloth.
Time:	15 minutes.

Gather together 15–20 everyday objects (such as a teaspoon, stapler, watch, CD, toothbrush). Try to ensure that they don't fall into obvious categories. Place them on a tray or table and cover with a cloth. Explain to the children that they will be shown some objects. No further explanation is necessary at this stage.

1 Arrange the group so everyone can see the objects, then tell the children that they have just one minute to look at what's on the tray. Uncover the tray.

2 When the minute is up, cover the objects on the tray with the cloth. If possible, arrange it so that no clues are given from the shapes under the cloth.

3 Without their seeing, remove one item from the tray and ask the children to look at the tray for another minute.

4 Can anyone spot which item has been removed?

5 Ask for a couple of volunteers to try to remember as many objects as they can – how many can they remember?

6 Now ask the rest of the group to jot down or sketch as many objects as they can remember.

7 How many can they remember? Most will be unlikely to remember any more than ten.

8 Explain that our short-term memories are unable to hold much more than about seven items at a time. If we re-ran the activity with only about seven items on the tray, more people would remember them. If we then took one of these seven away, most people would know which one had been taken.

💬 Imagine what life would be like if we only had a short-term memory. We would only be able to remember things that were happening, as they happened. Every day we would have to introduce ourselves to each other at school because we wouldn't remember who was who!

So how do we remember things for longer than a few minutes? We need to make sure we can rely on long-term memories. We are able to remember things for longer if they are linked to something else or if we can attach importance to them in some way.

Variations

As a variation of the 'What's missing?' part of this activity, you could ask the children to have a good look at what's in the room and then hide/remove something from it. How many can name the object that has been removed? You could even ask one of the group to leave the room and see how many of their classmates realize who is missing! Or perhaps you could do something different from usual – wear a hat, put your coat on – and see who notices.

Workshop

'The more you link, the more you learn.'

Jeannette Vos

U.F.A. Let's Learn How to Learn

Activity 4: **Making associations**

Aim:	To show how linking aids memory.
Resources:	Three unrelated objects (different from those used for the 'What's on the tray?' activity).
Time:	5–10 minutes.

This is a quick-fire activity. Ask the group to look at the three objects you place before them and then to try to find a way of linking them. They can discuss in pairs or threes how they linked the objects. For example, if your three objects were a roll of sticky tape, a glass and a newspaper, possible links might be: they are all manufactured; they are all round or have round parts to them (the newspaper could be rolled up); they are all often found in my classroom.

Use random objects – don't try to find three things that obviously link together; the children will find ways of linking them. Some might link them according to shape, material, use or even by making up a story!

Association, or linking, is one of the ways our memory holds on to information. We need to be able to link things to each other in order to remember them more easily. There will be many different ways of linking the same three objects. Some may seem obvious to some people, but not to everyone. This shows the individuality of our brains and how we see the world differently from other people, so we can all make different links between the same things.

Workshop

Memory

One, I listen or look with care,
Two, I repeat to myself what's there.

Three, I try another way,
Touch, or do, or see, or say.

Four, with something else I link,
This reminds me, when I can't think.

Five, I group or put into line,

And so I make the idea MINE!

U.F.A. Let's Learn How to Learn

Activity 5: **Chunking to remember**

Aim:	To show how making links between things can improve our recall.
Resources:	Word cards (pages 207–209) – one set for each small group.
Time:	15 minutes.

Ask the group to look at the words you give them and then work out a way of linking some of them to make it easier to remember. If after five minutes they haven't realized the link, explain that the words fit into one of six categories (food, families, stationery, electrical, feelings and clothing).

Once the groups have figured out what the categories are and have sorted the information, ask them to test themselves by turning the cards face down and trying to jot down as many words as they can from the list.

How many did they manage to remember?

Ask them to think back to the 'What's on the tray?' game and what we know about the amount of information we can store in our short-term memory. Did we improve on remembering seven items? If so, why? How?

Categorizing – making associations (links) between things – helps us to remember. Most children probably tried to remember the categories and that there were five words in each. Then all they had to do was remember five things – easy!

Workshop

Making the learning stick

Five easy steps to success!

1 Learn a topic.

2 Repeat within 24 hours.

3 Repeat again for 10 minutes at the end of the week.

4 Repeat again for 10 minutes two weeks later.

5 Repeat for 10 minutes one month later.

Be a successful learner!

U.F.A. Let's Learn How to Learn

Activity 6: **Brain teaser! Random letters?**

Aim:	To show the power of linking.
Resources:	None.
Time:	5 minutes.

This is another quick-fire activity. Tell the group that you will be reading out a series of letters and that you want them to remember as many as possible. Read the letters out clearly and steadily, then ask the children how many they can remember.

☛ D G B F I M K J E A L N C H

Now read the following list of letters and, again, ask the children how many they can remember.

☛ A B C D E F G H I J K L M N

How many people remembered more the second time? Did they realize that the letters were actually the same? It just shows the power of linking – the second list was linked together into a pattern that we are all familiar with – the alphabet.

Workshop

Help your memory

Making a mental picture is something everyone can do.

Visualizing is using your mind's eye, mind's ear and mind's feelings to remember – it's multisensory.

It's a mental movie.
It will improve your memory.
Try it!

Try visualizing!

U.F.A. Let's Learn How to Learn

Activity 7: **Remembering some more**

Aim:	To show the power of our memories.
Resources:	None.
Time:	5–10 minutes.

This activity follows on from the first activity in this workshop, but takes it a step further. Ask the group to think of a really positive memory and to picture it in detail. It must be a specific memory and of a time when they were really happy.

Ask them to try to visualize their memories in detail (they may find it easier with their eyes closed). You can help them by guiding their thinking and asking them to answer the following questions in their heads:

- Where were you?
- Who was there?
- What can you see?
- What can you hear?
- What can you smell?
- What can you feel?
- What can you taste?

Allow some time between each prompt for the children to follow their thoughts and picture the scene in their mind's eye.

Afterwards, ask the children to open their eyes when they are ready.

Memories are powerful – some of the group may have even been smiling as they remembered. Ask them to reflect on what they were thinking about, either with a partner or by themselves:

- How real was the memory?
- What details could you remember?
- How were you able to conjure it up – even though you were sitting here?

Positive memories are very powerful and can be a really good way of trying to make ourselves feel happy and relaxed, especially when we are feeling sad or tense. It's good to have a memory that we can use in this way. Perhaps the children could use the one they have just remembered as their positive memory?

Workshop

Family challenge

I've been learning about mnemonics. Do you know any?

We've been learning about the loci method for remembering things. Can I show you how it works?

Can I show you the memory tool I've made?

Take it home – let's learn together!

U.F.A. Let's Learn How to Learn

Part 2: **Workshop plan**

By the end of this workshop children will have:

- explored some more strategies for making their learning stick

- taken part in some experiments to show how their memories work.

The big idea

You can improve your memory – and here are some strategies to help!

Activity 8: **I'm X and I like to ...**
(minimum of 15 minutes)

Activity 9: **Loci method – using a person to remember things**
(20 minutes)

Activity 10: **Mnemonics**
(10-plus minutes)

Activity 11: **Create your own memory tool**
(30 minutes)

Family challenge

Take it home – let's learn together!

! *Don't forget to experiment with brain breaks (see page 13) – either at the start of the session or after about 20 minutes.*

Boost your memory:

mind map your learning.

U.F.A. Let's Learn How to Learn

Activity 8: **I'm X and I like to ...**

Aim: To show how repetition and mime are useful memory tools.

Resources: Circle of chairs.

Time: Depends entirely on group size and speed, but allow at least 15 minutes.

This warm-up activity is simply a variation on the game, 'My mother went to market and she bought …'. Ask the group to sit in a circle and think of one thing they enjoy doing that they would like to share with the group. As well as telling the group, they will also need to think up a mime or action to go with the information. For example, the first person might say: 'I'm Sarah and I like to laugh.' Sarah mimes laughing, then the whole group does the mime as well.

The game builds up with the next person introducing the first person: 'This is Sarah and she likes to laugh [this person does Sarah's laughing mime and the whole group copies], and I'm Manjit and I like to draw.' Manjit mimes drawing and the whole group copies the mime.

Carry on until the whole group has introduced themselves, starting with the first person's introduction each time. It soon becomes apparent that the people at the end of the cycle have many more names and mimes to remember, but they get more practice as they hear the information being repeated.

At the end ask the children which they found easier to remember, the information or the mime? We remember things if we are actively involved, so they probably remembered the mime more than the information.

Some scientists believe in a theory called 'muscle memory'. Our bodies remember how to do things, even without our consciously thinking about them, for example, riding a bike or throwing a ball. In fact, if we thought too hard about how to do these things, it might put us off.

Workshop

"We remember that which interests us."

Sigmund Freud

U.F.A. Let's Learn How to Learn

Activity 9: **Loci method – using a person to remember things**

Aim:	To introduce the concept of location (loci) as a powerful way of remembering things.
Resources:	Ten unrelated objects (see examples below).
Time:	20 minutes.

One of the most powerful ways of remembering things, devised during Roman times, the loci method works on the basis of linking objects to places or people that you know well – even world champions use this technique!

Show the students a range of about ten objects and give them a couple of minutes to see how many of them they can remember. It doesn't matter what objects you use, but examples are:

Item   1 – cup and saucer

Item   2 – elastic band

Item   3 – rolled-up newspaper

Item   4 – telephone

Item   5 – cheese roll

Item   6 – pink shoe

Item   7 – bunch of flowers

Item   8 – furry teddy bear

Item   9 – three glasses

Item 10 – paperclip

Ask the children to imagine a person they know very well (this could be a teacher, a parent or even themselves). First, they visualize the person they are going to use – for this exercise we will assume the children are using themselves.

1   Imagine the cup and saucer (**first item of any list**) on the top of your **head**.

2   Imagine the elastic band (**item 2**), which has grown to gigantic proportions, is pasted on to your **forehead**.

3   The rolled-up newspaper (**item 3**) is stuffed up your **nose**.

4   The telephone (**item 4**) goes in your **mouth**.

5   A cheese roll (**item 5**) can clearly be seen inside your **throat**, which you can visualize as a transparent cylinder.

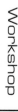

Workshop

Everyone can improve their memory!

U.F.A. Let's Learn How to Learn

■ Activity 9: **Loci method – using a person to remember things** *(continued)*

💬 **6** A pink shoe (**item 6**) is stuck to your **left arm**.

7 A bunch of flowers (**item 7**) is dropped on to your **chest**.

8 A cute furry teddy (**item 8**) is tied to your **belly button**.

9 Three glasses (**item 9**) are balanced on your **right foot**.

10 A huge glittery paper clip (**item 10**) is placed under your **left foot**.

Visualize the item you want to remember in or on a particular part of the body. Always do this in the same sequence, starting with the top of the head. There's no need to concentrate or try to remember. As long as you visualize clearly, your brain will do the rest. Now see how many of the objects you can remember.

We have only used ten items for this activity, but there are many other parts of the body you can use. Don't forget you can exaggerate the size of objects. The funnier or more unusual the image, the more memorable it becomes. Just as the throat was made transparent, so other parts of the body can be given similar treatment.

Using your imagination and making a picture in your head can really help your memory. Imagination is memory's friend!

✏️ *Points to make*

✓ The most important principles of the loci method are that you use something you already know very well (a person, your route to school, your home) and link it to the things that you want to remember.

✓ By visualizing your memory and making it as vivid and bizarre as possible, you're more likely to remember it.

Variations

1 Another well-known loci method is to visualize a journey you know well (perhaps the children could use their journeys to school) and think of the main landmarks along the way. You can then link the things you need to remember to each of the landmarks.

2 An alternative is to use the rooms in your home as the loci.

Workshop

My Clap, Run, Hop spelling memory

Colour

Colour helps your brain to remember patterns in spelling.

Linking

Join letters together using simple sentences. For example, remember how to spell the word 'said' using the sentence 'silly Ann is dancing'.

Actions

Using movement or actions helps you to remember.

Pictures

Your brain loves pictures and can remember them more easily than words.

Review

Going over your spellings regularly helps to move the spelling from your short-term memory into your long-term memory.

Unusual

Anything that is exaggerated, unusual or funny is easier to remember because it stands out as being different.

Noise

Saying things out loud helps to remind you of the sound of the word. Even giving silent letters a sound will help to remind you that they need to be included in the spelling.

Hidden words

Finding words within words helps to chunk down the spelling into smaller pieces that are easier to remember.

Order

Use numbers to help you order the letters of the spelling.

Patterns

Look for similar sounding words as they often contain the same pattern of letters.

Activity 10: **Mnemonics**

Aim:	To introduce a strategy that works especially well for learning spellings.
Resources:	None.
Time:	10–30 minutes, depending on whether you spend time creating new mnemonics.

Mnemonics are really just another way of chunking, using initial letters. Many children and teachers will already use them for remembering key information in a particular order, such as spellings. For example, to help you remember the spelling of the word 'because' you could remember the following sentence: 'Big elephants cannot always use small entrances.'

B ig
E lephants
C annot
A lways
U se
S mall
E ntrances

Or to remember the order of the planets from the Sun – Mercury, Venus, Earth, Mars, Jupiter, Saturn, Uranus, Neptune, Pluto – use the sentence: 'My very easy method just speeds up naming planets.'

M y
V ery
E asy
M ethod
J ust
S peeds
U p
N aming
P lanets

Ask the children about other mnemonics they already know.

Can they think of a good mnemonic for some words to do with memory: 'memory', 'association' and 'linking'?

Workshop

One collar and two sleeves are *necessary* to make a shirt!

Activity 11: **Create your own memory tool**

Aim:	To help the children synthesize what they have learned so far.
Resources:	Paper, glue, coloured pencils/pens and any other items to help create a poster; summary of the information on memory (*see below*).
Time:	30 minutes.

The idea here is for children to reflect on what they have learned about memory and put it into a form that will enable them to access the information as they need it. You may want to give them some of the information again, or let them use the task as a review activity in itself, and so concentrate on what they have learned and what they can remember from the rest of the workshop.

💬 Create a memory tool that will help you remember how to use your mega memory. It might be a poster, a song, a rhyme or a combination of these. Whichever you decide, make sure you include the following information:

● We remember information more easily if we can chunk it down or put it into categories.

● We remember things by linking them.

● Making things colourful helps us to remember.

● We remember things when they stand out – if they are exaggerated, bizarre or if we have strong feelings attached to them.

Workshop

What have I learned?

Where can I use my learning?

What could I do differently next time?

U.F.A. Let's Learn How to Learn

microwave	paper
T-shirt	happiness
uncle	felt-tip pen
coat	Gameboy
love	glue

Activity 5

tomato	stapler
anger	hat
brother	radio
cheese	sock
ruler	computer

rice	mother
fear	TV
ice cream	niece
joy	potato
shoe	auntie

Activity 5

'Mind mapping is really going to help me.'

UFA student

Mind mapping magic!

'I liked the mind mapping because I love doodling, and it will help me with work in school at the same time!'

UFA student

U.F.A. Let's Learn How to Learn

Introduction

They [mind maps] automatically inspire interest in the students, thus making them more receptive and co-operative in the classroom.

Tony Buzan, *The Mind Map Book*

Mind mapping is a brilliant thinking and learning tool originally developed by Tony Buzan. He believes that, rather than thinking in straight lines, our thoughts take us all over the place, making many varied connections that radiate in all directions. Mind mapping reflects the way we think and learn. The combination of colours, pictures and words is immediately appealing and memorable, and it compliments our brain's natural way of working.

Mind mapping gives us the Big Picture, showing how everything relates to everything else as well as giving the detail. We know that most children need to know the context of learning, and the Big Picture aspect of mind maps addresses this. The process of creating a mind map requires the learner to really engage with the learning on many levels, which appeals to most children.

Mind maps can be used to:

- record a lot of information in a small amount of space
- generate new ideas and organize them at the same time
- plan for other tasks, including writing
- aid memory.

It is important to try to stick to the rules of mind mapping, at least to begin with, in order to exploit the full potential of mind maps as a tool for thinking, learning and memory. The main aim of this workshop is to familiarize the children with these rules.

Six rules of mind mapping

1. Only use plain paper (lines on the paper distract the eye and do not allow you to read the mind map quickly).

2. Use landscape paper. Our horizontal peripheral vision is greater than our horizontal vision. Using the paper in the landscape format also means writing can be the right way up.

3. Begin with a central image. While you are drawing this, the brain is pre-processing relevant information for the rest of the map.

4. Thick branches radiate from the centre. Use a different colour for each. Each thick branch can represent a main part of the topic. Branches become thinner as they reach the edges, as finer details are added.

5. Single words (or very short phrases) should be printed clearly *along* the length of the line, not just at the end.

6. Use pictures, symbols, illustrations, and so on. These are used to create memory associations.   We remember images far more readily than words – it is said that a picture speaks a thousand words.

'I thought it was going to be boring, but it wasn't.'

UFA student

U.F.A. Let's Learn How to Learn

Introduction *(continued)*

The radiant nature of mind maps means you can add to any of the branches at any time. If you come to a standstill on one line of thought, carry on with another – your brain will continue processing the first subconsciously. That's the magic of mind mapping!

Like any skill, mind mapping needs practice, and Part 2 gives children the chance to have a go at mind mapping for themselves rather than working as a group. As their confidence grows, they will begin to develop their own style of mind mapping and see a multitude of uses for mind maps.

66 *They [mind maps] stimulate active thinking, develop cognitive skills of analysis, categorization and synthesis, and provide a visual means of communication and evaluation.* 99

Robert Fisher, *Teaching Children to Learn*

Family challenge

I've been learning to mind map. It's colourful and fun!

Let me teach you how to mind map. You'll find it useful, too!

When would you use a mind map?

Take it home – let's learn together!

U.F.A. Let's Learn How to Learn

Part 1: **Workshop plan**

By the end of this workshop children will have:

- seen and read a mind map
- worked out the rules of mind mapping
- had a go at mind mapping with the support of others.

The big idea

- We think and remember by connecting things, making associations and linking.
- Mind mapping combines all the elements that our brains need, which is why it is such an effective tool.

Activity 1: **This reminds me of …**
(15 minutes)

Activity 2: **Let's look at a mind map**
(10 minutes)

Activity 3: **Let's mind map together**
(25 minutes)

Activity 4: **Let's catch our learning!**
(10 minutes)

Family challenge
Take it home – let's learn together!

!

- *Using the rules, children could teach a member of their family to mind map. The topic is the family member themselves. All the family mind maps can be displayed in the classroom.*

- *Don't forget to experiment with brain breaks (see page 13) – either at the start of the session or after about 20 minutes.*

" Mind maps are a really neat way of parcelling up your learning on one page. I like making them and I think they're useful. They really help me to remember – pages and pages of notes put me off revision. These won't. "

UFA student

U.F.A. Let's Learn How to Learn

Activity 1: **This reminds me of ...**

Aims:	• To become aware that we often link and connect things together when we are thinking.
	• To reinforce the relationship between words and pictures.
Resources:	You may want to photocopy the activity sheets (pages 237–238) for students to work on. Alternatively, you could read out each statement and just ask the children to respond on plain paper.
Time:	15 minutes.

This is a quick-fire warm-up activity where the children actively think about their thought connection process. Remind them that in this case spelling and perfect drawing are not important, and that there are no right or wrong answers.

A list of memory trigger words (below) can be used for this activity, and you can add your own to the list if you like. The list deliberately includes both concrete examples and abstract ideas so that the children can experience making links with both.

💬 Write some words or draw a picture of whatever comes to mind when you hear (or read) the following memory trigger words:

- favourite game
- friend
- good feeling
- magic
- dangerous animals
- tool
- maps
- being lost

Divide the children into pairs. Ask the children to explain the connection to their partner by filling in the blanks in this sentence: 'This reminds me of .... because..........' For example, thinking of a favourite game, a child might link and respond by saying, 'This reminds me of football because we always play it at lunchtime and it's great fun.'

◼️▤ *Points to make* ════════════════➤

✓ Our brains connect and link everything together, with one thing reminding us of another, making a chain of information.

✓ Everything reminds us of something else; this will be different for each person.

Workshop

Tens of thousands of students around the world right now are taking notes. They are writing words down line by line, but the brain doesn't work like that – it stores information by patterns and associations. So the more you work with your brain's own memory method, the easier and faster you will learn.

Gordon Dryden and Jeannette Vos
The Learning Revolution

U.F.A. Let's Learn How to Learn

Activity 2: **Let's look at a mind map**

Aims:	● To give children the opportunity to look at a mind map.
	● To introduce the rules of mind mapping by giving children the chance to work out the rules for themselves.
Resources:	Either give the children individual copies of 'Jordan's summer holiday' mind map, or display the mind map on a whiteboard or overhead projector. The mind map can be found on the CD-ROM in full colour, or on page 239 in black and white; however, it is important that colour rather than black and white copies of mind maps are used to introduce the concept.
Time:	10 minutes.

Put up 'Jordan's summer holiday' mind map on the OHP, or give out copies. Give the children one minute to look at the map and get as much information from it as possible.

Turn off or cover the OHP or ask the children to turn their copies over, then ask them to try and remember as much information as they can from the mind map. What can they remember? You and they may be quite surprised at the amount of information that is being recalled. Let the children look at the mind map again – which bits did they remember and which did they forget?

Now ask the children to 'play detective' and work out the six rules of mind mapping: the six points that all mind maps have in common (see page 213). This can be done as a whole group or you may choose to ask the children to work in smaller groups and feed back their answers.

Briefly recap by mentioning all the rules and explaining how they are brain friendly.

◢▌▌ *Points to make* ▬▬▬▬▬▬▬▬▬▬▬▬▬▬▬▬▶

✓ Your brain loves colours; your brain loves pictures; your brain loves words. But what it loves even more is to put all these together; this is what a mind map does.

✓ Mind maps can contain a lot of information that is easier to remember than reams of writing.

✓ You need to use the rules of mind mapping to release the real magic of mind maps.

Workshop

Super learners ask super questions!

U.F.A. Let's Learn How to Learn

Activity 3: **Let's mind map together**

Aim:	To build on the rules for mind mapping by using a kinesthethic approach; children work in groups to support their understanding of the skills required.
Resources:	This activity needs significant preparation in advance. Draw and cut lots of large mind map arm shapes out of a stiff material such as lino or card, and paint in a variety of colours (large sheets of paper will work just as well but are not quite so durable). The central image can be either a painted object or just a picture printed, laminated and cut out. Keywords for the main branches also need to be printed and cut out; for example, if 'school' is the main topic, the keywords could be: 'teachers', 'lunchtime activities', 'events', 'feelings', 'friends', and so on. Some keywords are included but you may want to add others of your own. The children will also need plain A3 paper and coloured pens for their own mind maps.
Time:	25 minutes.

Using a large enough space, lay out the central image on the floor and randomly place at least four or five arms around it. Explain to the children that the group is going to mind map a very familiar topic – their school – represented by the central image. You might ask them what they would use as their central image if they were drawing this mind map.

Next, the group needs to decide what key areas the mind map could include. Show the children the range of keywords, pictures and objects you have already prepared. Ask individuals to pick up a cut-out keyword, picture or object of their choice and place it on an arm of the mind map. Often, children will place words at the end of the arm; if this happens, ask the group to think back to the rules (see page 213) and remember where the words should go. It is important that the word is placed along the length of the arm.

Once the whole group identifies the main branches, individuals can then either complete the mind map on paper or small groups can work on the larger mind map, taking an arm each. This approach gives them an initial structure and also allows them to get physically involved.

Alternatively, if the weather is good, you may want to use the playground to create a giant mind map using chalk, where groups of students can work on individual arms. A more permanent mind map can be created on huge sheets of lining paper pinned on to a smooth wall.

At the end of the session, encourage the children to think about when they might use mind mapping in and out of school.

▪▪ *Points to make* ▬▬▬▬▬▶

✓ Words must sit along the length of the arm.

✓ Words and pictures work together to give meaning, so both need to be chosen carefully.

Workshop

Colour
Pictures
Words
+ Fun

= Memorable mind maps!

Activity 4: **Let's catch our learning!**

Aim:	To help the children review their learning and give them an opportunity to articulate what they know.
Resources:	Photocopies of the partially completed mind map (page 240).
Time:	10 minutes.

Let the children know at the outset that this activity will help them with their Family challenge.

Individually, the children fill in the partially completed mind map, summarizing the rules of mind mapping. They can add more branches if they want to. Colour should also be introduced to the mind map.

Ask the children to pair up and compare their mind map with a friend. Encourage them to notice any similarities and differences.

The final minute is an opportunity for individuals to revise their mind map if they wish.

Workshop

Family challenge

I've been learning to mind map. Can I tell you what I like about it?

I want to practise mind mapping. Tell me what I was like when I was little and I'll make a mind map.

When else could I use mind mapping at home?

Take it home – let's learn together!

U.F.A. Let's Learn How to Learn

Part 2: **Workshop plan**

By the end of this workshop children will have:

- revisited the rules of mind mapping
- tried mind mapping for themselves
- used their mind map to share information with other people.

The big idea
We have to practise using the rules of mind mapping in order to make the most of this tool.

Activity 5: **Word association**
(10 minutes)

Activity 6: **Discovering keywords**
(10 minutes)

Activity 7: **Mind mapping from text**
(25 minutes)

Activity 8: **Catching our learning!**
(10 minutes)

Family challenge
Take it home – let's learn together!

> **!** *Don't forget to experiment with brain breaks (see page 13) – either at the start of the session or after about 20 minutes.*

Your brain loves pictures and different colours.

Mind maps are a really *good* way to help you remember things because they use many of your skills and they're fun.

You'll learn faster when you're having fun!

U.F.A. Let's Learn How to Learn

Activity 5: **Word association**

Aim:	To illustrate how our brain links ideas together in a chain of connected words. Often, the final word seems totally unconnected to the original word, but our brains have found associations that have lead to that point.
Resources:	None.
Time:	10 minutes.

This warm-up game is a fun activity that can be played either as a whole class or in smaller groups.

Begin with a trigger word. You may want to use a specific set of trigger words but any will do. Each person takes it in turn to add a word that they associate with the previous one only. At any time, someone else can challenge the association, so that the person has to explain how they have come to that connection.

This game can go on forever, so you may want to limit the number of words added, depending on the size of the group. Small groups of five can work on multiples of five.

Here's an example of how the last word can be so different from the first:

Flower → stem → break → glass → drink → lemonade → advert → television → news → war.

For an extra challenge, groups could give their trigger word and tenth association word to another group, which then has to see if it can work out a chain of associated words that link the first and last word. For example, another group would be given the task of figuring out how to get from 'flower' to 'war'.

This game gets easier with practice and can be returned to again and again.

Workshop

❛The mind mapping is such a relief – it gives me a way of sorting out the masses of information I have. It makes revising it all seem possible!❜

UFA student

U.F.A. Let's Learn How to Learn

Activity 6: **Discovering keywords**

Aims:	● To focus children's attention on identifying the essential information that needs to be captured.
	● To encourage children to use fewer, more carefully chosen words when mind mapping.
Resources:	None.
Time:	10 minutes.

In each sentence below there are keywords – the words that give the sentence most of its meaning. Write the following sentences on the board and ask the children in pairs to decide which is the most important keyword (to be coloured in one colour) and the second and third most important keywords (to be coloured in other colours).

- I love all sweet things, especially chocolate.

- In my garden there are many colourful plants.

- The best thing about my bedroom is the huge bed.

- Brains love colours and pictures.

- I have cats, dogs and fish as pets.

You may want to add sentences of your own to those suggested.

Now ask the children to try to represent the sentence visually as a mind map branch using their key words (see examples below).

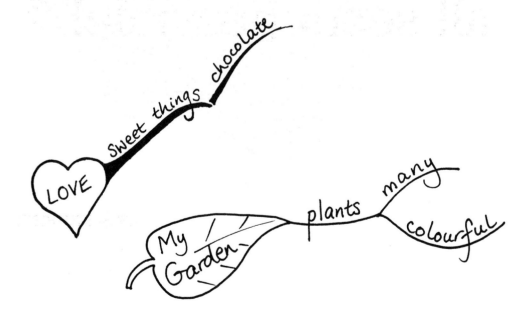

Workshop

'As a result of today I'm going to mind map my homework activities.'

UFA student

U.F.A. Let's Learn How to Learn

Activity 7: **Mind mapping from text**

Aims:	● To give children the opportunity to see how information can be synthesized from a linear form into a mind map.
	● To give children further practice with mind mapping.
Resources:	A piece of text of your choice, ideally some non-fiction, photocopied for each child; plain paper and coloured pens.
Time:	25 minutes.

Give out the blank sheets of paper and photocopied text to each child, and explain that they're going to create a mind map based on this piece of text. You can either read through the text with the children, or let them read it for themselves.

Now ask the children to draw a picture that represents the main topic, starting in the middle of the blank, landscape page. If there happens to be illustrations on the photocopied sheet, they can copy or cut these out and use them in their mind maps.

In pairs, ask them to work out and write down the keywords from the text, which will go on the main branches of the mind map.

They can then continue to mind map in pairs, groups or individually, as they wish, adding as much detail as they can from the text given.

Workshop

Use mind maps to:

- ● record information

- ● plan a story

- ● plan a presentation

- ● revise from.

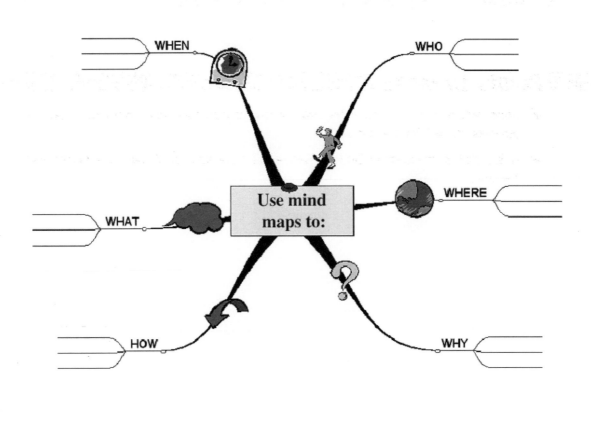

Activity 8: **Catching our learning!**

Aim:	To give children the opportunity to consider a range of uses for mind mapping.
Resources:	None.
Time:	10 minutes.

This activity can be done in small groups or as a larger group. Sitting in a circle, ask the children to collect some of the different uses for mind mapping. Each child should be able to answer the question: 'When can you use mind mapping?' Encourage children to articulate their answers using the following sentence stems, which can be written on the board.

- Mind mapping can help me to…

- I can use mind mapping to…

- Mind mapping will be useful when I have to…

- I am going to mind map when…

💬 You could also ask:

- Has anyone said anything you had not thought of?

- What else would help you develop your ability to mind map?

Points to make

✓ Mind mapping can be used for many different purposes, from planning a talk in assembly to revising for exams.

✓ It is a skill that needs to be practised – the more you mind map, the better you become.

Workshop

Trees remind me of mind maps! What else reminds you of mind maps?

U.F.A. Let's Learn How to Learn

Write some words or draw a picture of whatever comes to mind
when you think of the following memory trigger words:

Favourite game

Friend

Good feeling

Magic

Activity 1

Write some words or draw a picture of whatever comes to mind when you think of the following memory trigger words:

Dangerous animals   **Tool**

Maps   **Being lost**

Activity 2

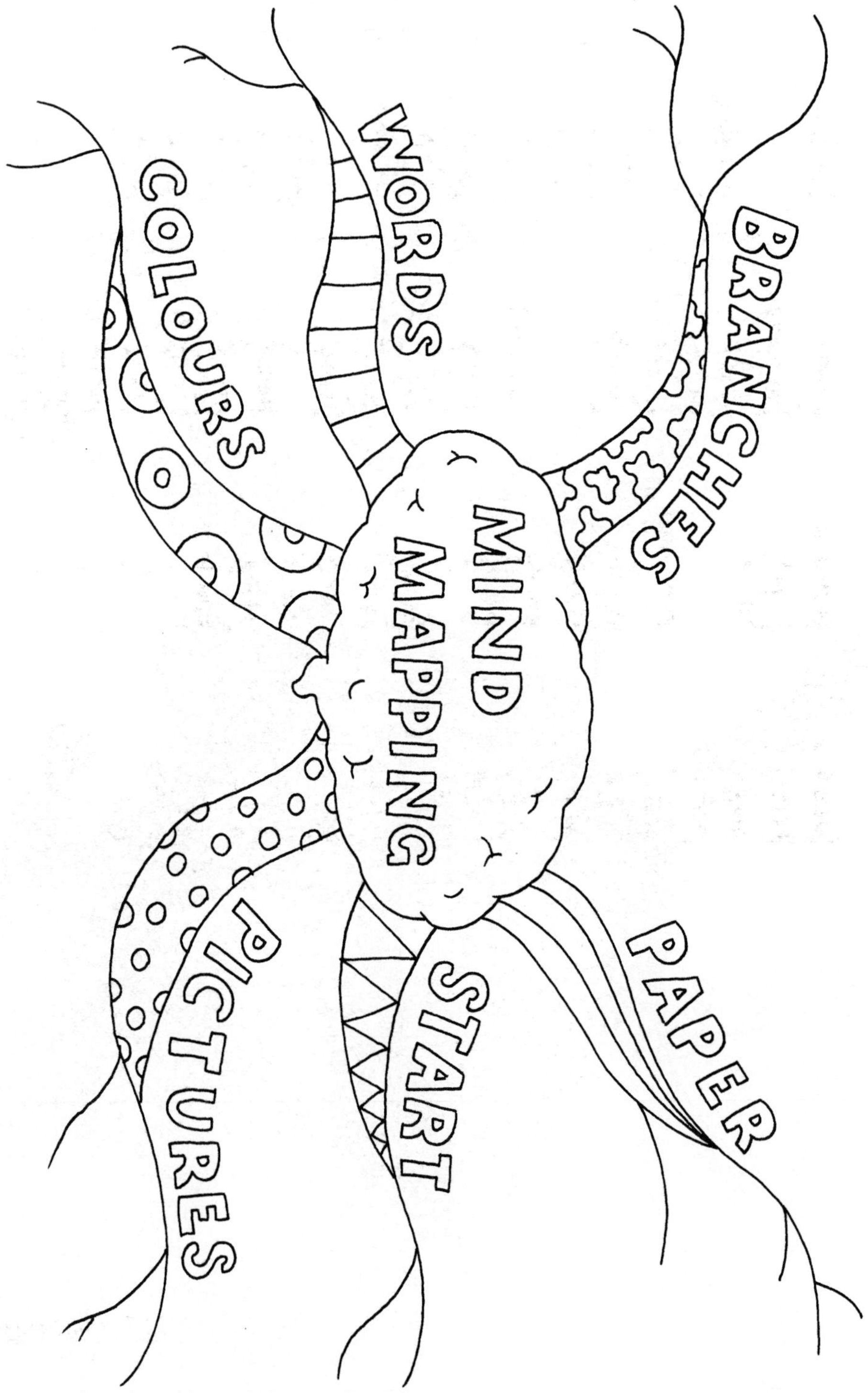
MIND MAPPING
BRANCHES
WORDS
COLOURS
PICTURES
START
PAPER

'I found out that learning is fun and interesting.'

UFA student

'Can we have a day like this every day?'

UFA student

U.F.A. Let's Learn How to Learn

Super Learning Days

Imagine a day:

That's all about learning to learn;

Where staff try out new things;

Where children realize they are intelligent;

Where there is a tangible sense of fun;

That has an impact a week, a month, a year down the line.

Imagine a Super Learning Day!

U.F.A. Let's Learn How to Learn

Introduction

What is a Super Learning Day?

We have been developing Super Learning Days (SLDs) since the UFA started in 1996. Since then, they have grown from learning to learn days, where children and young people began to think about *how* they learned rather than *what* they learned, to days that model much of what is now known as accelerated learning. For our partner schools across the country, SLDs provide an opportunity for staff development as well as a space where children and young people can try out new ideas and actively learn about themselves as learners in a fun way.

School is all about learning – but sometimes a day focused on how the brain works and how we learn best can really help to boost children's confidence in their learning. SLDs give children the opportunity to recognize that they learn in different ways and that they have particular intelligence strengths which they can use to learn more effectively and retain new knowledge for longer, both in and outside school. A successful SLD empowers children to take control of their own learning and gives teachers the opportunity to explore brain-friendly approaches to learning.

SLDs give the children a day off-timetable, a day that focuses entirely on exploring how they learn and/or giving them a multisensory experience of learning. It offers children the opportunity for sustained immersion in activity, focusing on learning to learn. A day like this lends itself to doing things in creative new ways, such as grouping children differently or focusing on healthy eating.

This is a great opportunity for children and staff to learn alongside one another. It is important that staff have the opportunity to familiarize themselves with the materials and the research that underpins them. A training day for the staff that focuses on brain-friendly approaches to teaching and learning would be ideal, allowing staff to explore new approaches to learning: the day itself then provides a safe space in which to experiment. Children take part in a day that is different from their everyday experience of school, and which highlights skills that will have a significant impact on their learning both inside and outside school.

The day should not be regarded as a stand-alone experience for children or staff, but rather a catalyst for further development, and ways of extending the impact of the day should be seized.

A typical Super Learning Day timetable

8.15	Healthy breakfast for children and teachers in the canteen.
8.45	Assembly with a difference: setting the tone for the day.
9.15	Morning session: carousel of three activities, plus break time.
12.30	Healthy lunch for children and teachers in the canteen, with games.
1.15	Assembly hall: re-focus.
1.30	Afternoon session: activities in small groups.
2.45	'Show what you know' session: presentations by the groups.
3.30	Staff evaluation.

Imagine a day

Rena's story describes a typical UFA Super Learning Day. Her experiences draw on a number of successful Super Learning Days that have taken place in UFA partner schools across the country.

It's early and already there's a tangible feeling of excitement in the air. Teachers rush around – that's not unusual – but today they are excited about the learning. A few early birds loiter in anticipation in the playground, one clutching his mum's hand. Both know that today is going to be something special, something important and they are curious to find out more. The excitement mounts as the entire year group gathers outside the canteen where they are going to register. They use the posters on the wall to work out which group they will be working with today.

Rena notices that in her group there will be a number of teachers and some names she doesn't immediately recognize. She will later discover they are sixth form peer tutors from the nearby secondary school and some parent helpers. Rena is in the Red Wizard group and she collects her identifying sticker as well as a black and white UFA T-shirt. The letters UFA remind her of the previous week's assemblies and the numerous teaser posters that have been dotted around the school.

The smell of warm toast invites the children into the canteen where groups of friends chatter animatedly in the queue to get their breakfast. Colourful posters, some created by other children, remind Rena why she needs to eat breakfast to help her to make the most of her learning time at school. She sits with her friends and some teachers, and conversation flows easily over cornflakes.

The assembly hall is filling with a sea of black and white T-shirts and background music creates an inviting atmosphere. Teachers, parents and helpers all sit together and, at times, it is difficult to tell who is who. A series of slides, each one representing a famous face with the question 'Intelligent?' underneath, prompt the audience into articulating their reaction. 'Oohs' and 'aahs' of recognition ignite numerous conversations as to whether that person is intelligent or not. The music begins to fade as assembly begins.

The assembly invites lots of audience participation as everyone explores some simple brain facts by taking part in a game of 'Stay standing if ...' The potential of the brain is illustrated by volunteers making up the number 100,000,000,000, and a challenge is set for the children to find out what that number is. Other children are used to explore the structure of the brain and to illustrate the idea of whole-brain learning. Volunteers use mimed actions to represent various parts of the living brain.

The children leave, collecting a bottle of water as they go. They can drink from this throughout the day. The carousel of workshops in the morning session begin.

In the 'My mega memory!' workshop, Rena discovers many ways to improve her memory. She is shown a range of objects and tries to remember them randomly. Then she is encouraged to try out the suggested techniques of association, linking, story telling and visualization to improve her recall. At regular intervals she takes sips of water to help maintain her concentration.

Around the walls are posters that encourage, stimulate and remind her what they are doing. Background music creates a calming atmosphere. The peer tutors help by making sure everyone is involved and occasionally they suggest an idea. Everyone manages to achieve success in something.

Rena moves on to the next workshop, which is called 'The power of positive thinking'. Here she works alongside adults and friends on a number of collaborative and individual tasks, prompting her to think about the importance of having an 'I can' attitude towards her learning. They are all discovering new things about themselves.

The final session of the morning, 'Mind mapping magic', begins like all the others with brain breaks to focus everyone's attention. A giant mind map is partially created in the middle of the room. Rena suggests a word for one of the main branches and she places the giant word along the arm. The children then divide into smaller groups and complete the mind map on paper.

Lunchtime is an opportunity to catch up with friends in different groups over a healthy lunch. Rena usually has a packed lunch and today her dad has responded to the letter that was sent home the previous week by packing a healthy, energy-packed lunch. Peer tutors run some games throughout the lunch hour, which the children may join in with if they want to. Rena doesn't usually like games, but the laughter is infectious and she joins in with the tug of war.

After lunch everyone gathers once more in the hall for a bit more activity, using some Tai Chi movements. Rena is re-focused on the learning. Everyone divides up again, this time into much smaller groups of between 6 to 10 children working with an adult and a sixth form helper. They fill in a questionnaire that helps them to find out how they learn. Everyone finds out more about the different ways in which they like to learn. Rena discovers that she is quite a visual learner and that pictures, diagrams and mind maps are really good tools for her to use.

The penultimate activity of the day is for each group to prepare a presentation to 'Show what you know'. They have the choice of preparing a poster, poem, song, rap or role play to illustrate some of the important learning from the day. Rena's group have fun making up a rhythmical poem about what a brain needs to work properly.

Once again the hall fills with excitement as everyone gathers together, eager to show their work. There are a series of newly created posters, displayed around the hall. Some posters are three-dimensional and very tactile. Groups show their work and the learning from the day is celebrated. Teachers and sixth formers perform alongside the children, and there is a mixture of drama, music and poetry. The energy levels are still high as the day draws to a close. Rena puts all her energy into the final power clap.

Some children are reluctant to leave and they linger in the hall to chat a little more. Thanks are exchanged. Rena happily clutches her Super Learning Day booklet, where she has recorded information from the day, and her 'Family challenge' sheets. She is looking forward to sharing her ideas from the day with the rest of her family as well as her mum who has been helping out. 'I'm going to try this out with your brother tonight' is her mum's parting shot as they leave.

So what does a Super Learning Day look like?

Super Learning Days (SLDs) can take many forms. Most schools begin by running a generic learning to learn day, focusing on workshops that explore the skills and personalization of learning. However, many schools are now experimenting with running days that embody these learning to learn processes but with a specific emphasis. This might be a day focusing on revision skills, or it might be an enrichment day where staff run workshops that move away from the curriculum taught within the normal school day. Days like this highlight the learning process and encourage children to reflect on how, as well as what, they have been learning. Many schools run SLDs for a whole year group, while others focus on specific groups of children. Some schools even run whole-school SLDs and experiment with vertical grouping.

The day usually starts with an active assembly. Children then move around a series of workshops before coming back together at the end of the day to share what has been achieved. Depending on the way children have been grouped, it may be important to have a short workshop at the beginning of the day to do some team-building and agree some group ground rules for the day. This is especially important where the children have been organized into 'teams' for the day, perhaps led by an older student as team leader or peer tutor. There is also often a review workshop built in at the end of the day for children to reflect on and evaluate what they have learned, and to think about how it might help them in the future. Super Learning Days for older children may include three or four workshops, whereas younger children often have several more, shorter workshops.

Beginnings and endings

An active assembly is very important as it gets the day off to a positive start and sets the tone for staff and children. Usually, the assembly is around 20–30 minutes long and could use some of the activities in the 'My amazing brain!' workshop. This is also an opportunity to register children in their newly formed groups.

It is useful to bring everyone back together at the end of the day. This can be a very short, 10-minute assembly that celebrates what has been achieved, perhaps displaying some images, words or outcomes from the workshops. However, if there is time, it can also include feedback from different workshop groups.

Workshops

Any of the workshops in this book may be used to create a learning to learn programme for the day, and they do not need to be presented in a particular order. However, while a Part 1 workshop may be run as a stand-alone unit in its own right, a Part 2 workshop often builds upon the activities and knowledge gained in Part 1. Staff can decide to run one workshop and present it to a number of different groups throughout the day, or deliver a range of different workshops for a particular group. It is useful to plan and, if possible, facilitate workshops with a colleague. This way the day works as a staff development day as well as a day for the children, and it is important that staff are developing and refining new skills and knowledge in teaching and learning. It is also useful if the day can end with a review of the activities, where the children can reflect on what they have done and take part in an activity that will help to link the SLD with their learning in the future.

Super Learning Day booklet

Many schools collate materials needed to support the workshops into a booklet for the children. In addition to workshop resources, this booklet might include a programme of the day, evaluation sheets, and so on. It is a useful way of raising the profile of the day and is especially valuable if the booklet incorporates things that the children can take away and use in their long-term learning.

Team debrief

At the end of the day it is important to give the staff team time to reflect, review and evaluate the day. This need not take long, but it is a good opportunity to find out how the day has gone for them. Further evaluation with staff and young people is useful too.

Follow-up

One of the potential dangers in running SLDs is that they may be seen as a one-off experience, both for staff and children. Coming back to the day in assemblies and lessons after the event helps to extend the impact of the day by keeping it in everyone's mind. This allows children to practise and consolidate skills learned during the day, and to build them into their personal 'toolkit for learning'.

Planning a Super Learning Day

This section outlines the steps involved in organizing a Super Learning Day and looks at some of the issues a school will need to think about. These will form an important part of the training day you facilitate with your staff.

1 Decide on the outcomes.

- How will you know the day has been a success?
- How will staff and children evaluate the day?

The outcomes could link to a specific school development action plan or other decisions around teaching and learning.

2 Decide on the shape of the day.

- Will the timings stay the same or be different from the normal school day?
- Will the day start with breakfast?
- Which workshops will you use and how long will each workshop be?
- How will you start and close the day?

The shape of the day will contribute significantly to making the day different and special. As with the workshops chosen, it needs to reflect the desired outcomes for the day.

Avoid trying to pack too much into the day and making the workshops too short, as this can lead to frustration if there is little opportunity to think and reflect. If the groups have been restructured, you may want to consider an opportunity to do some team-building early on in the day.

You also need to consider the shape of the day for staff as well as for the children. It is useful to have a short briefing session for the staff before the day begins. This helps to create a team approach and provides an opportunity to share any last-minute changes, instructions or to address any worries. The plenary session for tutors to share their thoughts at the end of the day is very important as it can provide valuable insights into the outcomes of the day and how these can be built upon for future events.

3 Decide how to group the children and adults.

- Which group of children is the day focused on (year group, mixed year group, and so on)?
- How will the children be grouped?
- How will the adults be grouped?
- How will the day build a group ethos?

Changing groupings for the day makes it interesting and different for everyone, and allows the children to establish new relationships by working with people they may not have worked with before. Where possible, the ratio of staff to children should be at least 1:15–20. This allows for more movement and a more intimate atmosphere. However, changing groups can mean some children feel a little insecure, so there needs to be an element of team-building in the day and a way of setting ground rules for groups to operate in. School staff will be the best judges of appropriate groupings for the day.

4 Decide how to let everyone know about the SLD.

- How will the right expectations of the day be created in advance?
- How will you raise awareness about the day with children, staff and parents?

Marketing the day properly is significant to the success of the event. It is vital that children have the right expectations of the day and look forward to it with anticipation and curiosity. It is important that children and staff realize the day is about learning and trying out new approaches, as well as having fun. This will help them to evaluate the day more effectively; they may come to the conclusion that learning can be enjoyable if you take an appropriate approach.

Informing and involving parents, governors, other staff, the press, and so on, all help to raise the profile of the day and make it a special event. The language used to market the day needs thinking about carefully so the purpose is clear to all involved.

5 Decide on the role of staff members.

- What training is required to ensure that staff feel confident to facilitate the workshops?
- Who will do what – are there enough people to enable staff to work in pairs?
- Who else could be involved? Parents? Governors? Lunchtime supervisors? Local businesses? Community groups?
- Will you use peer tutors/sixth form helpers? Will they need training?

The more people that can be involved in the delivery of the day, the better the experience will be for all. Where tutors are able to work in pairs, the professional development for both is doubled; tutors are more likely to take risks with their approaches if they have the support of another. Also, having two people means that there are increased opportunities to stand back, watch and reflect on what is happening. Preparation is shared too, so the pressure on tutors is minimized.

Involving learning support assistants, governors, parents, peer tutors, and so on, as part of the extended learning team, means that messages from the day are spread further, thus extending its impact. It also reinforces the message that everyone is a learner and a teacher. Extending the learning team to include peer tutors or sixth formers gives the children very positive role models and makes the day feel different. It is important for peer tutors to take part in training in order to carry out this role. Some older children could form a news team to report on the day and perhaps produce a newsletter or a display of what has been achieved.

6 Decide where in the school to run your SLD.

- Which areas of the school can be used for the day?
- Who will be responsible for the rooms that will be used?
- How might the room layout be changed so more active activities can take place?
- How can rooms be made more brain friendly?

7 Decide how you will extend the impact of the SLD.

- How will the staff team follow up the day?
- How will the children follow up the day?

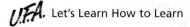 Let's Learn How to Learn

8   Decide how to evaluate the day.

- What evaluation tools could you use to try to gauge the effectiveness of the day for staff and children:
  - On the day itself?
  - In the longer term?

Ideas for making the day different

Here are some of the ways schools have tried to make a Super Learning Day different:

- Invite the children. Give every student an invitation to the day, presenting them with an overview and what they can expect to get out of it.
- Children come in non-uniform.
- The day has a theme.
- The day begins with a healthy breakfast.
- Only healthy, brain-friendly food is served on the day.
- Children are given their own bottle of water to drink whenever they need it.
- Children are grouped completely differently from the usual groupings.
- Staff are included in the groupings and take part in the learning, too.
- Groups are given names, for example, from a popular work of fiction.
- Lunchtime sports and games activities are run by peer tutors.
- Parents, governors and other guests are invited to take part in the day.
- Digital photographs taken during the day are shown during the closing assembly and displayed in the foyer.
- Children and staff display what they have learned in the closing assembly.
- A theme song is used to open and close the day.
- A teaser poster campaign is used in advance of the Super Learning Day to spark interest and curiosity.

Case Study 1: **Manchester UFA network**

Introduction

Eleven primary schools in Manchester were involved in running whole-school Super Learning Days on the same day. All 11 schools are part of the UFA partnership in Manchester, and UFA Fellows from the schools worked together to plan the day. The Fellows had been working towards this event for two terms, and had also involved their staff in training for the day.

Aims of the day

The schools worked together to run a big learning to learn event in Manchester. Each school had its own aims, but all were focused on actively involving the children in learning about learning.

On the day

About 4,000 children from 11 primaries were involved in a variety of learning experiences, both at their own schools and at other inspiring venues, including the local library, the Museum of Science and Industry, the cathedral and a local football club.

The SLDs were different in every school – as we would expect them to be – with every school stamping its own mark on the day. While each school opted for a learning to learn focus, some also decided to have their own themed day, with the Willows School running a two day back-to-back event with a popular fiction theme. Several schools had 'news teams' to capture the learning events as they unfolded and creating newsletters to send home to parents.

Many of the schools made links with their local secondary schools, and KS3 pupils were involved as peer tutors; some also gave support to the news teams. Parents and other members of the local community – including the Lord Mayor, sports personalities and MPs – were also involved.

Throughout the event, all the children were involved in activities that helped them to think about how they, as individuals, were learning and what that meant for their schoolwork. Many schools used the day as a springboard for a range of out-of-hours activities running throughout the week.

Highlights

Some children had the opportunity to extend their Super Learning experience with a residential stay at Ghyll Head Outdoor Education Centre in the Lake District. Here they took part in a number of Multiple Intelligence Challenges that had been organized. In addition, the local library held a poetry workshop, with an appearance and readings by an actual poet! There was a tangible feeling of excitement from children and adults alike.

'A real boost for teaching and learning in schools across the city.'

Mick Waters, Director of Education, Manchester

'A brilliant day! I'm not sure who enjoyed it the most –
me or the children!'

Teacher

Case Study

'Every child had a smile on their face all day. The whole
school was buzzing!'

Teacher

'At first I was a bit nervous but after five minutes it was fantastic!'

Pupil

Case Study 2: **West Lea School, Edmonton, London Borough of Enfield**

Introduction
West Lea is a special school in Edmonton in the London Borough of Enfield. Pupils have a range of medical conditions, and, since September 2002, it has been designated as a school for children with complex needs (whereas before it was a school for delicate children). Some pupils start at the school at the age of four. Others come later from other special schools or from mainstream education. Where appropriate, pupils are integrated into mainstream education on a part-time basis initially, with a view to full-time integration if it is successful. Pupils can stay at West Lea until they have completed Year 12, having taken GCSEs and other qualifications.

Aims of the day
The main aims of the day were to raise awareness among pupils, staff and parents about different learning styles; to raise the self-esteem of pupils, particularly underachievers; and to celebrate individuals' strengths.

The school improvement plan highlighted the need for fresh ideas and approaches to teaching and learning as an area for development. As part of this plan, the Super Learning Day provided a way to improve the quality of teaching and learning in the school by putting the UFA principles into practice and sharing the approaches with staff and pupils. A staff INSET day was key to helping them achieve this. They worked with other schools locally who had already run their own UFA Super Learning Days, and then ran three twilight training sessions for staff to ensure that everyone was comfortable with the programme.

On the day
The day involved the whole school, with the children taking part ranging from five to 17 years old. Workshops focused on learning styles, problem solving and mind mapping. Some of the primary classes used the story *Big Sarah's Little Boots* by Paulette Bourgeois and Brenda Clark (Scholastic) as a focus for exploring their learning. The staff arranged a picnic and several VAK-based activities at lunchtime, including an energetic dressing up race and a cryptic 'match the sound to the object' game.

Highlights
At the end of the day each child received a certificate and told the staff what they had got out of the day. The lunchtime activities and picnic also went down really well. Caroline Pickard who led the organization of the day said, 'The highlights for me were seeing the pupils enjoying themselves and the activities being a success.'

> *'More than 100 children aged 5-17 joined in the event, which introduced different ways of learning through problem-solving activities.'*
>
> Local newspaper

Case Study

'This is the best day ever!'

Pupil

'I found out that I could help others and achieve myself.'

Pupil

'At the end of the day this is an event which is fun for the whole school community and very worthwhile.'

Headteacher

Children get creative at Norwich Road Primary School

Case Study 3: **Norwich Road Primary School, Norfolk**

Introduction

Norwich Road is a primary school in the heart of Norfolk. It was part of the Thetford education action zone and is now a member of the Thetford excellence cluster. A foundation school with 480 pupils aged between three and 11, it has been actively working with the UFA for five years. As a result of a forward-thinking headteacher and senior management team, the school has developed SLD Challenges that take place every term, with teams combining for peer tutoring.

Aims of SLD Challenges

These vary according to the age of the children and the needs of the particular teams. However, all Super Learning Day Challenges encompass the firm belief that a multisensory approach to teaching is essential, that brain-friendly learning is the most effective and that it must be challenging and fun. The school wanted to create more opportunities for speaking and listening skills, and incorporate this with problem-solving activities as a team.

Example of a SLD Challenge

On Monday, the children assembled together in the hall for a brief introduction and discussion about what the SLD Challenge was about. Norris, the school bear, talked with the children about how to be brain friendly and what the brain needs for optimum learning. The children then built a living brain and learned what effect each part of the brain has on their learning.

The children were then divided into four workshop groups: Biff, Chip, Floppy and Kipper. They went off to their workshops to see what was in store for them. The Year 2 children 'buddied' a Year 1 pupil. Some of these children were just over five years old! The children rotated through all the workshops over four days, experiencing a different style of learning in each. All the workshops gave the children different types of brain exercises and used music.

The event kicked off for Years 1 and 2 with a week-long SLD Challenge based around 'That's the way to do it'. The SLD Challenge provided children with opportunities to investigate how to put on a puppet show, through problem solving. The workshops were designed and planned collaboratively by four members of staff to ensure that VAK and multiple-intelligence learning were at the heart of them. The workshops also matched a variety of learning intentions for English, mathematics, science, design technology, art and design and information technology. Every child spent a day in each workshop, experiencing playwriting, advertising, theatre- and puppet-making.

Plays were written and scripts produced. Programmes, tickets and posters were designed to advertise the event, puppet theatres built and a variety of puppets from marionettes to stick puppets were constructed according to the characters in the plays. The atmosphere was intense and electric. On Friday morning we rehearsed and practised the scripts, then in the afternoon we performed to the Nursery, Reception and the rest of the infants. Throughout the week children evaluated their work through 'ladders of success'.

 Let's Learn How to Learn

At the end of each day the children reflected, evaluated and celebrated their achievements. At the end of the Challenge they reflected on the week with an evaluation and learned how to anchor their successes.

Highlights

As the week went by it was noticeable how, in just a short space of time, the children's independence increased. Given the right environment, they learned to experiment, discover and take risks. There was a lot of co-operation, understanding and support. It was difficult to identify those with special needs; they all contributed to discussions and produced equally successful work. The real highlights were the sense of achievement and pride on the faces of young children who had been given such a demanding challenge.

'It was lovely to hear that they had enjoyed themselves and that they had found things out about the way they learn.'

Teacher

'I never thought I could speak in front of all the infants. This week has given me so much confidence in myself.'

Pupil

We did it! It was a challenge to make a puppet in a day, from planning a design to the finished article.

U.F.A. Let's Learn How to Learn

Recommended reading

Bowkett, Stephen (1997), *Imagine That...*, Network Educational Press, Stafford.

Bowkett, Stephen (1999), *Self-Intelligence*, Network Educational Press, Stafford.

Brierley, Michael (2001), *Emotional Intelligence in the Classroom*, Crown Publishing, Bancyfelin.

Buzan, Tony (1993), *The Mind Map Book*, BBC Books, London.

Call, Nicola with Featherstone, Sally (2003), *The Thinking Child*, Network Educational Press, Stafford.

Call, Nicola and Smith, Alistair (2000), *The ALPs Approach* and *The ALPs Approach Resource Book*, Network Educational Press, Stafford.

Caviglioli, Oliver and Harris, Ian (1999), *MapWise*, Network Educational Press, Stafford.

Dryden, Gordon and Vos, Jeannette (2001), *The Learning Revolution*, Network Educational Press, Stafford.

Fisher, Robert (1995), *Teaching Children to Learn*, Nelson Thornes, Cheltenham.

Fogarty, Robin (1997), *Brain Compatible Classrooms*, Skylight Professional Development, Glenview, Il.

Hannaford, Carla (1995), *Smart Moves*, Great Ocean Publishers, Arlington, Va.

Hoffman, Eva (2002), *Introducing Children to Mind Mapping*, Learn to Learn, Middlewich.

Hoffman, Eva (2002), *Introducing Children to their Senses*, Learn to Learn, Middlewich.

Jensen, Eric (1996), *Brain-Based Learning*, The Brain Store, San Diego, Ca.

Jensen, Eric (2000), *Learning with the Body in Mind*, The Brain Store, San Diego, Ca.

Lucas, Bill and Smith, Alistair (2002), *Help Your Child to Succeed*, Network Educational Press, Stafford.

Margulies, Nancy (1995), *Map It!*, Zephyr Press, Tucson, Az.

Prashnig, Barbara (2004), *The Power of Diversity*, Network Educational Press, Stafford.

Smith, Alistair (2000), *Accelerated Learning in Practice*, Network Educational Press, Stafford.

Smith, Alistair (2002), *The Brain's Behind It*, Network Educational Press, Stafford.

Smith, Alistair (2002), *Move It*, Network Educational Press, Stafford.

Useful websites

www.alite.co.uk	Alistair Smith's site
www.brainconnection.com	Brain Connection site, 'Brain Science in Plain English'
www.campaign-for-learning.org.uk	Campaign for Learning site
www.childrenthinking.co.uk	Philosophy With Children in schools in the UK
www.dialogueworks.co.uk	Philosophy for Children site
www.dfes.gov.uk	Department for Education and Skills site
www.edwdebono.com	Edward de Bono's site
www.eqi.org	Emotional Intelligence site
http://faculty.washington.edu/chudler/neurok.html	Neuroscience for kids site
www.Mckergow.com	Mark McKergow's site
www.mind-map.com	Tony Buzan's site
www.mindjet.com	Mind mapping site
www.networkpress.co.uk/lsa	Information about Learning Styles Analysis on the Network Press site
www.pzweb.harvard.edu	Project Zero site (Educational research group at the Graduate School of Education, Harvard University)
www.sapere.net	Society for the Advancement of Philosophical Enquiry and Reflection in Education site
www.teachingthinking.net	Robert Fisher's site
www.thingkingcap.org.uk	Philosophy for Children site
www.ufa.org.uk	University of the First Age site